Joyce's Visible Art
The Work of Joyce and the
Visual Arts, 1904–1922

Studies in Modern Literature, No. 38

A. Walton Litz, General Series Editor
Consulting Editor for Titles on James Joyce
Professor of English
Princeton University

Other Titles in This Series

No. 5	*Studies in Joyce*	Nathan Halper
No. 10	*Inverted Volumes Improperly Arranged: James Joyce and His Trieste Library*	Michael Patrick Gillespie
No. 13	*Hamlet and the New Poetic: James Joyce and T.S. Eliot*	William H. Quillian
No. 15	*The Sources and Structure of James Joyce's "Oxen"*	Robert Janusko
No. 23	*James Joyce and the Beginnings of* Ulysses	Rodney Wilson Owen
No. 27	*The "Ithaca" Chapter of Joyce's* Ulysses	Richard E. Madtes

Joyce's Visible Art
The Work of Joyce and the Visual Arts, 1904–1922

by
Archie K. Loss

UMI RESEARCH PRESS
Ann Arbor, Michigan

Copyright © 1984
Archie Krug Loss
All rights reserved

Produced and distributed by
UMI Research Press
an imprint of
University Microfilms International
A Xerox Information Resources Company
Ann Arbor, Michigan 48106

Library of Congress Cataloging in Publication Data

Loss, Archie K. (Archie Krug)
  Joyce's visible art.

  (Studies in modern literature ; no. 38)
  Revision of the author's thesis—Pennsylvania State
University, 1970.
  Includes index.
  1. Joyce, James, 1882-1941—Knowledge—Art. 2. Art
and literature. I. Title. II. Series.
PR6019.O9Z7163 1984   823'.912   84-2657
ISBN 0-8357-1576-0

Contents

List of Illustrations   *vii*

Acknowledgments   *xi*

1 Introduction: Joyce and the Visual Arts   *1*

2 The Iconography of the Earlier Work   *7*

3 *Ulysses,* Cubism, and Other Movements in Modern Art   *41*

Illustrations   *69*

Notes   *109*

Bibliography   *121*

Index   *125*

List of Illustrations

1. Édouard Vuillard. *In Bed.* 1891. Oil on canvas. Musée d'Orsay (Palais de Tokyo), Paris   *69*

2. Édouard Vuillard. *Mystery.* c. 1895. Oil on board. Private collection, New York   *70*

3. Roberto Basilici. *On the Tiber.* c. 1900-1910. Present whereabouts unknown   *71*

4. Aristide Maillol. Illustration to Vergil's *Eclogues.* (Published Weimar: Cranach Press, 1925)   *72*

5. Ferdinand Hodler. *Spring.* 1901. Oil. Museum Folkwang, Essen   *73*

6. Ferdinand Hodler. *Youth Admired by Women.* 1903. Oil. Kunsthaus, Zürich (on loan from the Gottfried Keller Foundation)   *74*

7. Ferdinand Hodler. *Distant View.* 1906. Oil. Present whereabouts unknown   *75*

8. Edvard Munch. *Melancholy.* 1901. Color woodcut. Munch Museum, Oslo   *76*

9. Edvard Munch. *The Lonely Ones.* 1899. Color woodcut. Munch Museum, Oslo   *77*

10. Max Klinger. *The Philosopher.* 1910. Etching. Staatliche Graphische Sammlung, Munich   *78*

11. Emile Bernard. *Self-Portrait (Vision).* 1891. Oil. Present whereabouts unknown   *79*

12. Meyer de Haan. *Self-Portrait.* 1890. Oil. Present whereabouts unknown   *80*

13. Paul Gauguin. *Te Po (The Great Night).* 1894. Woodcut. (First published in 1921)   *81*

14. Edvard Munch. *Death in the Sickroom.* 1895. Oil. Munch Museum, Oslo   *82*

15. Rudolf Jettmar. *The Poet.* Etching. Present whereabouts unknown   *83*

16. Alphonse Mucha. Printed velvet design. c. 1900.   *84*

17. Robert Burns. *Natura Naturans.* 1891   *85*

18. Dante Gabriel Rossetti. *Astarte Syriaca.* c. 1867. Drawing. Present whereabouts unknown   *86*

19. Odilon Redon. *Closed Eyes.* 1890. Musée d'Orsay (Palais de Tokyo), Paris   *87*

20. Edvard Munch. *Madonna.* 1895. Color lithograph. Munch Museum, Oslo   *88*

21. Paul Gauguin. *Breton Eve.* 1889. Pastel and aquarelle. Marion Koogler McNay Art Museum, San Antonio   *89*

22. Edvard Munch. *Man's Head in Woman's Hair.* 1896. Color woodcut. Munch Museum, Oslo   *90*

23. Gustave Moreau. *Apparition.* Cabinet des Dessins, Musée du Louvre, Paris   *91*

24. Edvard Munch. *Woman.* 1899. Color lithograph. Munch Museum, Oslo   *92*

25. Édouard Vuillard. *The Wood.* c. 1892. Oil. Collection Mr. Alexander Lewyt   *93*

26. Paul Sérusier. *Incantation.* 1890. Oil. Present whereabouts unknown   *94*

27. Edvard Munch. *The Voice.* 1893. Oil on canvas. Museum of Fine Arts, Boston   *95*

28. Moritz von Schwind. *The Organic Life of Nature (Das Organische Leben der Natur).* Drawing   *96*

29. Giovanni Segantini. *Evil Mothers.* 1894. Oil. Kunsthistorisches Museum, Vienna   *97*

30. Albert Weisgerber. *Reclining Figure in a Mountainous Landscape.* 1914. Staatsgalerie moderner Kunst, Munich   *98*

31. Edvard Munch. *Winter.* 1899. Oil. Munch Museum, Oslo   *99*

32. Pablo Picasso. *Les Demoiselles d'Avignon.* 1907. Oil on canvas. The Museum of Modern Art, New York (Acquired through the Lillie P. Bliss Bequest)   *100*

33. Francis Picabia. *Picture Painted in Order to Tell, Not to Prove.* 1915. Pen and ink and gouache on tracing paper. Present whereabouts unknown   *101*

34. Juan Gris. *The Table.* 1914. Collage on canvas. Philadelphia Museum of Art   *102*

35. Georges Braque. *Violin and Palette.* 1909-10. Oil on canvas. The Solomon R. Guggenheim Museum, New York   *103*

36. Umberto Boccioni. *Unique Forms of Continuity in Space.* 1913. Bronze. The Museum of Modern Art, New York (Acquired through the Lillie P. Bliss Bequest)   *104*

37. Marcel Duchamp. *"L.H.O.O.Q."* 1919. Reproduction, altered by pencil. Private collection   *105*

38. Pablo Picasso. *The Window.* 1919. Gouache. Private collection   *106*

39. Marcel Duchamp. *Tu m'.* 1918. Oil and graphite on canvas (with objects). Yale University Art Gallery (Bequest of Katherine S. Dreier)   *107*

40. Giacomo Balla. *Study for the Materiality of Lights plus Speed.* 1913. Gouache. Collection Lydia Winston Malbin   *108*

Acknowledgments

One accumulates so many debts to so many different people in the course of doing a study like this one that it becomes impossible in the space of a few lines to acknowledge them all. Particular thanks, however, must go to the following: Robert W. Frank, Jr., Professor Emeritus, Department of English, The Pennsylvania State University; Professor George L. Mauner, Department of Art History, The Pennsylvania State University; and J. Mitchell Morse, Professor Emeritus, Department of English, Temple University.

Research and writing time for this project has come from a sabbatical leave from The Pennsylvania State University and also from a summer stipend from the American Council of Learned Societies, for both of which I have been quite grateful. Additional support has come from the Scholarly Activities Fund of The Behrend College of The Pennsylvania State University.

My most enduring thanks for the entire project, as for all I do, must go to my wife Suzanne.

For permission to quote from the works of Joyce, I am indebted to the following:

Viking Penguin Inc.: *Collected Poems, Dubliners,* and *A Portrait of the Artist as a Young Man;*

Random House, Inc.: *Ulysses*

The Society of Authors: *Dubliners, A Portrait of the Artist as a Young Man, Stephen Hero, Ulysses* and *Collected Poems*

The Bodley Head: *Ulysses*

Jonathan Cape Ltd.: *Chamber Music, Dubliners,* and *A Portrait of the Artist as a Young Man*

I also wish to thank Harcourt Brace Jovanovich, Inc., for permission to quote from "The Waste Land" from *Collected Poems 1909-1962* by T.S. Eliot. Portions of this study have appeared in *Journal of Modern Literature.*

1

Introduction: Joyce and the Visual Arts

"Beauty is so difficult"—this phrase of Aubrey Beardsley's which Joyce picked up from Yeats and then recorded in one of his early notebooks,[1] sums up the dilemma Joyce faced at that point in his early development when he decided that *Stephen Hero* had to be scrapped and the aesthetic problem which his story posed approached anew. In refining that approach, through note and draft, Joyce came increasingly to depend upon the evidence of the eye. He also came to render pictorial or visual images—his visible art—in terms familiar to one who grew up at the end of the nineteenth century. In so doing, he liberated himself from Stephen's problem, also described in the early notes: "He desired to be not a man of letters but a spirit expressing itself through language because shut off from the visible arts by an inheritance of servitude and from music by vigour of the mind."[2]

In translating the evidence of the eye, of the world he saw around himself, into the pages of his early work, Joyce used imagery common to both the literature and the painting of the *fin-de-siècle* and the turn of the century. Indeed, it does not go too far to say that, as Joyce's work throughout much of his life was fixed almost exclusively in subject matter and detail in the Dublin of his adolescence and young manhood, so was his visual imagery also fixed in the world of that time, so that ever afterwards, in spite of his ignorance of painting, his imagery reflected the *fin-de-siècle* way of seeing (if not always of interpreting) the world.

Instances of this correspondence in vision occur in descriptive detail on many levels throughout the earlier work and will be pursued in greater depth in chapter 2 of this book. For the moment a few examples will suffice. At the beginning of the third chapter of *A Portrait,* Stephen, sitting in the schoolroom at Belevedere as a December dusk falls, muses on supper and then on his night wanderings. As he sits there thinking of these discrete yet complementary objects of his growing appetites, something happens to the equation on the page of the scribbler before him:

> The equation... began to spread out a widening tail, eyed and starred like a peacock's; and when the eyes and stars of its indices had been eliminated, began slowly to fold itself together again. The indices appearing and disappearing were eyes opening and closing; the eyes

opening and closing were stars being born and being quenched. The vast cycle of starry life bore his weary mind outward to its verge and inward to its centre, a distant music accompanying him outward and inward. What music?... he recalled the words, the words of Shelley's fragment upon the moon wandering companionless, pale for weariness. The stars began to crumble and a cloud of fine stardust fell through space.(*P* 102-103)[3]

In this passage Joyce uses the same phrase that he used in "The Dead" for Gabriel's evocation of Gretta painted on the stairs: *"Distant Music* he would call the picture if he were a painter" (*D* 210).[4] Similarly, as Gabriel and Gretta are walking away from the house of the Misses Morkan, Gabriel, recalling words he had addressed to her some years before, thinks: "Like distant music these words that he had written years before were borne towards him from the past" (*D* 214). The phrase in "The Dead," like the phrase in *A Portrait,* suggests in good *fin-de-siècle* fashion a link between the creative process and music, though the more interesting, from the aesthetic standpoint, is the transformation in *A Portrait.* Stephen is not yet an artist, and the transformation the equation undergoes does not have, to the same degree as Gabriel's imagined painting, the form of a work of art, yet it is clearly the imagination of an artist, however undeveloped, that has gone to work on the equation, and the resultant transformation, however indecisive or wearying, is something more like art than Gabriel's painting.[5]

In any event, this transformation begins with the figure of the peacock's tail—the equation spreads "out a widening tail, eyed and starred like a peacock's"—an image which recurs with such frequency in the art of the *fin-de-siècle* as to constitute a motif: the abstract and exotic pattern of the peacock's feathers that achieved in English art of the 1890's its most famous representation the peacock skirt of Salomé in Aubrey Beardsley's illustrations to Wilde's play.[6] Another parallel to Beardsley's work—and another reference to the Salomé story—occurs later in *A Portrait,* in the description of Cranly as John the Baptist, with "the face of a severed head or deathmask, crowned on the brows by its stiff black upright hair as by an iron crown... a priestlike face, priestlike in its pallor, in the widewinged nose, in the shadowings below the eyes and along the jaws, priestlike in the lips that were long and bloodless and faintly smiling"(*P* 178). The phrase "lips...long and bloodless" provides a fair description of the lips of Iokanaan in one of Beardsley's illustrations to Wilde's play, and the phrase "widewinged nose" of the nose in another.[7] The image is appropriate to Stephen's view of Cranly at this point in *A Portrait,* as a rival for Emma's hand, and it is also, at least in terms of the deathmask image, common to the art of the *fin-de-siècle,* blending, as we shall later see, with the image of the artist in the painting of the period.

In another passage in *A Portrait*—during the composition of the villanelle—Stephen seeks to shelter himself from outer life so that the inner life of the imagination may flourish:

Introduction: Joyce and the Visual Arts 3

> The full morning light had come. No sound was to be heard: but he knew that all around him life was about to awaken in common noises, hoarse voices, sleepy prayers. Shrinking from that life he turned toward the wall, making a cowl of the blanket and staring at the great overblown scarlet flowers of the tattered wallpaper. He tried to warm his perishing joy in their scarlet glow, imagining a roseway from where he lay upwards to heaven all strewn with scarlet flowers. Weary! Weary! He too was weary of ardent ways.(*P* 221-222)

The cowl suggests monkish withdrawal from common life—the *vita activa*—into the *vita contemplativa*. The key word in the passage comes at the end—"Weary! Weary! He too was weary of ardent ways"—a word that occurs twenty-two times in *A Portrait*.[8] As in the transformation of the equation, here Stephen's imagination moves outward—in the proper direction—and then mistakenly back upon itself. The stress upon weariness—though providing a cross-reference to the villanelle and to other passages in the novel—also provides a heavy note of irony, because, of course, it is not by means of such weariness and retreat but by means of their opposite that Stephen is to achieve artistic and personal fulfillment. However much it keeps him from becoming the artist he would be, he is very much the child of the *fin-de-siècle* in his weariness, and conforms, in this respect as in others, to the type of the *poète maudit*.[9] A number of paintings done in the 1890's by Nabi painter Edouard Vuillard commemorate this attitude toward life so typical of the period, most notably perhaps the striking *In Bed* of 1891 (Figure 1), in which the sleeping figure is severely elongated and lies beneath a partially covered Crucifix.[10] Such figures in the iconography of *fin-de-siècle* art are related, like those of the deathmask, to the representation of the artist in the period.

These and other examples dealt with at greater length below show us the pervasiveness of such imagery in the early work of Joyce, a pervasiveness notable both for the importance such images have to the interpretation of that early work and also for their continuity in the later work, where they have less importance but still represent the same way of seeing. It is in *A Portrait*, however, that purely visual imagery has the greatest thematic importance, the climactic passage of each chapter of the novel depending heavily upon visual details of one kind or another. Thus, toward the end of chapter I, Stephen, on his way to the office of the rector of Conglowes, takes note of the paintings that line the walls:

> He passed along the narrow dark corridor, passing little doors that were the doors of the rooms of the community. He peered in front of him and right and left through the gloom and thought that those must be portraits. It was dark and silent and his eyes were weak and tired with tears so that he could not see. But he thought that they were the portraits of the saints and the great men of the order who were looking down on him silently as he passed ... (*P* 55)

Stephen responds to the faces that he meets—those of St. Ignatius Loyola, St. Francis Xavier, and the others—as traditional representations of figures of the

Church; this art is a product of the Church and Stephen's response to it is largely conditioned by his past servitude. Yet it is these pictorial images which help Stephen to see himself in a new light as he faces the rector, and it is significant in this regard that the paintings are *portraits:* full and finished renderings of heroes of the Church. Succeeding concluding passages—to chapter II, with the scene with the prostitute; to chapter III, with Stephen surrendering himself to the Host; to chapter IV, with his final surrender to all that the mortal angel on the beach represents to him; and to chapter V, as he sets forth on his journey—also rely heavily upon visual detail or visual effect to make their point.

However, the relationship between Joyce's work and the visual arts goes beyond that of mere imagery to include also that of technique and general aesthetic purpose. By technique, I refer to those methods by which an artist's vision is rendered on canvas or page.[11] By general aesthetic purpose, I mean similar though perhaps completely independent solutions to common aesthetic necessities. In the case of Joyce's work viewed in relationship to modern art, this common aesthetic necessity involves an increasing degree of tension between observed reality and ways of rendering it. This tension—definable at times in terms of greater and lesser degrees of realism, at other times still in terms of modes wholly alternative to realism—represents in the end the chief area of correspondence between Joyce's work and the visual arts of this century.

Correspondences between the techniques of Joyce's early prose and Impressionism have been noted.[12] There are also correspondences between the techniques of Joyce's early work and those of notable post-Impressionists or Symbolists, for example in chapter III of *A Portrait;* "The chapel was flooded by the dull scarlet light that filtered through the lowered blinds; and through the fissure between the last blind and the sash a shaft of wan light entered like a spear and touched the embossed brasses of the candlesticks upon the altar that gleamed like the battleworn mail armour of angels"(*P* 116). This technique of spotlighting occurs frequently in Nabi and Symbolist work. To achieve symbolic effect in a small and at first glance innocent interior (ca. 1895) (Figure 2), Vuillard uses the same device of spotlighting, reinforcing it with the title *Mystery*. In this tiny painting, light from a window falls on a lamp—with its associations of the eternal laws of existence to be found in *la vie quotidienne*, of which the Nabis made so much—and the light from the lamp (or from some mysterious source) picks out on the wall a Tau cross with its mystic associations, of which the Nabis also made much. (The cross in Vuillard's *In Bed*, because partially covered, also suggests the Tau.) In a similar manner, Joyce, in the passage from *A Portrait*, singles out on the altar the embossed brasses of the candlesticks with their associations of Church tradition and heroic Christianity which Stephen is ultimately to reject in becoming a priest of the imagination.[13] Such devices in painting—part of the general fragmentation of the object, beginning with Impressionism and culminating in Cubism, by which small and seemingly insignificant details increasingly give symbolic significance to a whole composition—correspond closely to the fragmentation of image and phrase, discernible in the work of Joyce and others, which led ultimately to the development of the narrative technique known as stream-of-consciousness.

That technique, along with the various narrative strategies which accompanied it and ultimately displaced it in Joyce's work by the end of *Ulysses,* also has numerous affinities to the main line of development of modernism in the visual arts—to Cubism (especially for collage and its intentional ambiguity in subject, time, and point of view), to Futurism (for its multiple temporal imagery and its dynamism), to Dadaism (for its playful aesthetic questions), and even to Surrealism (by extension of certain principles of Dadaism and the other movements). In short, Joyce's work, as it grows and develops, shows an increasing number of similarities to mainstream modern art—to the avant-garde as it has been defined, principally in the French tradition, in the history of art. These similiarities enrich our understanding of Joyce's achievement in the cultural history of this century, as well as our understanding of specific fictional techniques associated with his name. They are scarcely surprising, however, if we remember the milieu in which Joyce worked and the chronology of his work in compa[rison with modern] art and its immediate predecessors.

The 1890s were the formative years for much of Joyce's ca[reer], [through] and including *A Portrait.* It was during this time that he grew from the schoolboy increasingly aware of his own differences from others to the young man on the brink of the artistic career that was to change the course of modern fiction. The experiences of this decade—from the time Joyce was a student at Clongowes Wood College, which he entered in 1888, through his years at Belvedere College in Dublin, to his entrance, in 1898, of University College—form the basis of *Stephen Hero, A Portrait of the Artist as a Young Man,* and many of the stories later collected as *Dubliners.* By the end of the first decade of the new century, Joyce had acquired gradually the techniques necessary to the task he had set himself as a writer.

The period from 1890 to 1910 marked in the visual arts the high point of Symbolism and Art Nouveau and the gradual emergence, especially after 1907, of the basic principles of the movement which came to be known as Cubism. In the wake of French Impressionism, Symbolism presented a literary response to the phenomenal world which the Impressionists had striven to render in naturalistic terms; largely conservative in technique, it represented an alternative to Impressionist goals. Art Nouveau was in many respects a decorative version of Symbolism, prevalent more in the graphic arts and in the crafts than in the fine arts. With both of these tendencies Joyce's early work has much in common, especially in terms of imagery but also, in some instances, in terms of technique. It has also much in common with the subtle *bourgeois* Symbolism of Vuillard and the Nabi circle, who reached their peak in the early 1890s, and with the much more expressionistic Symbolism of the influential Norwegian artist Edvard Munch.

From 1910 to 1920, despite the decisive interruption of World War I, developments in the visual arts were rapid and revolutionary. Joyce was publishing his first books, and in 1918 *Ulysses* had begun to appear in serial form in *The Little Review* and *The Egoist*. In this decade, due largely to Cubism, most of the basic principles of painting established in the Renaissance and more or less adhered to by all artists since that time were overturned or at least seriously questioned, and those that remained untouched by Cubism or Futurism, the Italian movement which in some respects resembled Cubism, were dealt with after 1916 by the Dadaists and their program of anti-aestheticism. With most activity in Paris and elsewhere interrupted by the war, Zurich, where Joyce had moved with his family from Trieste in 1915, became, with the advent of Dadaism, the most important address in the world of art.

By 1920—when Joyce moved to Paris and *Ulysses* moved into its final stages—this was no longer the case. By the early 1920s painting had entered an *époque floue*[15] from which it was gradually to emerge with the development, later in the 1920s, of Surrealism and abstract art. In the early 1920s the vocabulary of Cubism and related movements had become common parlance and the principles of Dadaism were only beginning to be systematized in Surrealism. It was in this atmosphere of the triumph of one set of tendencies and the gradual emergence of a counter-set that Joyce moved to Paris, where Surrealism, under the guidance of André Breton, was just beginning to develop as a movement. By the end of the decade it was by far the most important movement in art—though it had by then shown itself to be so various as to cause serious questions about its unity—and Joyce had already begun to publish parts of the "Work in Progress" which later became the *Wake*. In the 1930s, Surrealism—by now politicized, shaken by internal disruptions, yet still so all-inclusive in its definition of itself as to challenge previously prevailing notions of the discreteness of the arts—continued to be the most important single movement in the fine arts. With the coming of World War II, however, its place was to give way to the inner visions of its more abstract proponents; all signs of these times seem now to have been pointing to this final triumph of pure painting.

The relationship between Joyce's work, as it developed, and these developments in art is complex and various, requiring a sense both of the limitations which must be respected in such an inquiry and of the possibilities such an inquiry affords. The imagery of the earlier work—in particular that of artist, girl, chamber and forest—give us the ocular proof to begin.

2
The Iconography of the Earlier Work

The imagery of Joyce's work—in particular the work up to and including *A Portrait*—has much in common with two different though related movements or tendencies in art at the end of the nineteenth century and the beginning of the twentieth—Symbolism and Art Nouveau. It is not unusual to find such relationships between the work of a major writer like Joyce and the visual arts of his period—one would expect to find in almost all cases certain common imagery and themes—but in Joyce's case the coincidence is remarkable because of the significance of this common imagery to his work. In *Dubliners* and *A Portrait* especially, major point after major point is made in visual terms best apprehended with a knowledge not only of the imagery of Symbolist poetry, but also of the imagery of Symbolist art. An examination in detail of certain key images tells us something not only about what Joyce saw in the world around him, but also how he saw it.

Symbolism and Art Nouveau

Arthur Symons, in *The Symbolist Movement in Literature,* did as much as anyone for the young Joyce's generation to define French Symbolism in literature for English-speaking readers. His definition of the Symbolist ideal as "a form of expression, at the best but approximate, essentially but arbitrary, until it has attained the force of a convention, for an unseen reality apprehended by the consciousness"[1] applies almost equally well to Symbolist painting, except that the Symbolist painters had to find visual equivalents for the "unseen reality" they attempted to express. They tried to make graphic the ineffable, to find plastic form for emotions and moods that words could only barely express, to give substance to shadows.

If the central tendency of painting in the nineteenth century was toward a naturalism best expressed in the work of the French Impressionists, whose fundamental goal was to capture light as the eye perceives it in the atmosphere, Symbolism represents a secondary, but no less viable tendency, to represent the images perceived by the mind's eye.[2] Stylistically and thematically diverse, Symbolism, which reached its peak of influence in the 1890s, grew out of

Romanticism and ultimately, at least in part, into Surrealism. Like Surrealism, it maintained close ties with literature from its beginnings. Its styles ranged from the naturalistic canvases of the German and Dutch painters connected with the movement to the semi-abstract style of the French Nabis, whose theorist, Maurice Denis, had asserted, as early as 1890, that "a painting—before it is a battle-horse, a nude, or a certain anecdote—is essentially a flat surface covered with colors and a certain connected order."[3] In subject matter the work ranged from the ideal to the bizarre, from the now rather quaint-looking allegorical canvases of Puvis de Chavannes to the misogynistic, scatological illustrations of Félicien Rops: the whole range of subject matter suggested by Baudelaire (who, with Wagner, was one of the key figures in the development of the Symbolist aesthetic) in "Spleen et Idéal."[4] The frequency of illustration by Symbolist painters and draughtsmen is in fact an indication of their literary ties, though these ties are often expressed in less obvious forms than in the art of illustration.

If illustration is encountered frequently in Symbolist art, it is, with the poster, the essential two-dimensional form of Art Nouveau. Sharing with Symbolism much of its imagery and some of its technique, Art Nouveau was a development primarily in graphic art and design, known as Jugendstil in the German-speaking countries. Its goal was not to elucidate the invisible forces that shape us (a "revolt," as Arthur Symons put it, "against exteriority")[5] but, rather, in the spirit of the English Arts and Crafts Movement, to improve the reality of the exterior world by introducing into it beautiful objects and designs.[6] In Art Nouveau, the bizarre is softened till it becomes the adolescent naughtiness of Aubrey Beardsley, and the ideal is hardened until it becomes the idea-less poster art of Alphonse Mucha. Yet this art of lines (some curvilinear, some angular) and flat surfaces, which carried over heavily into architecture and design, was ubiquitous in British and European art of the turn of the century. The parallels between Joyce's work and the art of this period are attributable as much to Art Nouveau—which, through magazine and public art, anyone of this time would know—as they are to the more arcane and, for Joyce, less accessible, Symbolist art. These parallels or similarities—to Art Nouveau or Symbolist art—also suggest certain sources or analogues in the literature of Symbolism, with which Joyce's earlier work shares many ideals and techniques.

Portrait of the Artist

In the famous section which forms the conclusion of chapter IV of *A Portrait*, Joyce brings together, in the character of Stephen and in the figure of the wading girl he sees, two prominent types from Symbolist painting and Art Nouveau—one the sensitive young man fearful yet desirous of immersion in the waters of life, the other the girl who symbolizes at least part of the life in which he would be immersed, or who serves to channel that life to him, a girl with long flowing hair and an innocent look. For neither type is this the first appearance in the work of Joyce. The girl appears in certain stories of *Dubliners* and before that in *Chamber Music*—not to mention the later *Exiles* and the earlier Epiphanies—and Stephen, or the type of which Stephen is representative, in those works and in *Stephen Hero* as well. Just as the girl shares certain qualities with characters who are seemingly quite different from her—for instance with Polly Mooney of "The Boarding House"—so Stephen shares certain qualities with such characters as Gabriel Conroy and James Duffy, both of whom in some respects are quite different from him. However much they may differ in age, in degree of imagination, or in human potential, Stephen, Gabriel and Mr. Duffy are alike in their narcissism, their passivity, their isolation, and their tendency—partly as a result of these qualities—to view life and themselves through a glass darkly. In this they, and the young man of the *Chamber Music* sequence, conform generally to the type of the *poète maudit*.

Stephen Dedalus, Stephen Hero, Gabriel Conroy, James Duffy, the young man of the *Chamber Music* sequence—these and other figures in the early work of Joyce have their visual counterparts in portraits of artists and in artists' self-portraits, as well as in more general work, in Symbolist art and in Art Nouveau. Thus, for example, in the case of Stephen and the young man of *Chamber Music*, there are several series of works depicting youths in relationship to water—works which suggest by this relationship spiritual or physical renewal, and also works which suggest quite the opposite: a narcissistic turning back upon oneself, as after staring too long at oneself in a mirror. Other works, depicting figures shut out from ordinary—and in some cases extraordinary—human activity, suggest parallels not only with Stephen and the young man of *Chamber Music*, but also with Gabriel and Duffy. The first of these gives us, as it were, a view of the artist's private role; the second a view of the artist's public role. Other works give us both. An etching by Roberto Basilici from the pages of the Munich publication *Jugend* provides us with an example of the first (Figure 3).

This work depicts in profile a nude youth, poised on the edge of rocks on the shore of the Tiber. One leg and one arm are raised, creating just enough tension in the youth's body to suggest that he is considering a leap. An etching by Hans Thoma, also from *Jugend*, presents us with a more spiritualized version of the same scene.[7] This work depicts a muscular nude youth, his feet nearly touched by the waves, sitting pensively on a bare shore and staring off into the distance. The volumes and the outlining of the figure suggest early Picasso; the subject and theme suggest not only early Picasso but also early Joyce. The title of Thoma's work—*Solitude*—provides a clue to the relationship: the subject is raised to the general by the suffix and partly by the very sparseness of the representation, which, though of a time, is timeless. The young man in the Nabi Jan Verkade's *By the Seashore* (1892)[8] lies at the left of the canvas and gazes introspectively in the direction of the sea on the right. Here the considered leap is entirely spiritualized; the figure lies motionless, in a state of meditation. In a woodcut by Aristide Maillol, one of a series of illustrations begun by the artist in 1912 for an edition of Virgil's *Eclogues* finally published in 1925 (Figure 4), the youth becomes a narcissist, drawn, with lines reminiscent of the curvilinear lines made popular by Art Nouveau, as if floating underwater or in the womb, his head bowed in sleep or in self-contemplation. Meditation here gives way to self-absorption; the dreamer becomes the dream. In another illustration to the *Eclogues,* Maillol's *Corydon Sees Himself in a Pool*[9], the narcissistic element is even plainer. The male figure in scenes of this sort—typically a young man, sometimes merely a boy—frequently shades into the androgynous type that occurs so often in the art of the 1890s and the turn of the century, for instance in the work of Beardsley. The work of Belgian sculptor Georges Minne provides a borderline case. His fountain of kneeling boys, their arms wrapped protectively around themselves, strongly conveys by repetition the helpless quality of all such figures. Their androgynous quality is a manifestation of their undefined inner state.[10]

Artists' self-portraits often trade on the same image. In 1902 Picasso protrayed himself as a contemplative figure looking at the sea in a drawing in which he lies with his back to the spectator and holds a palette and brushes in his left hand.[11] In a similar drawing of his painter friend Junyer in profile on a beach, the renewal implicit in many such scenes becomes explicit, the forms of the landscape suggesting, or growing into, the forms of naked women and, in the center background, the head of a man. The scene suggests imaginative activity—perhaps anticipatory to artistic activity—in a decidedly parodic manner.[12]

The works thus far discussed suggest various parallels with Stephen on the beach—Stephen, alone and isolated, leaning toward the sea as the youth in Basilici's *On the Tiber* leans toward that river, but resisting the plunge, remaining passive and undefined as Minne's kneeling boys, or self-centered as the Corydon of Maillol's illustration; Stephen, perhaps mocked by Joyce as Junyer is perhaps mocked by Picasso (the wading girl, like the sterile bird-women that were the sirens, has "long slender bare legs... delicate as a crane's and pure" and a "bosom... as a bird's, soft and slight" (*P* 171). But most interesting, perhaps, in relationship to Joyce's work, is a group of paintings done by the Swiss painter Ferdinand Hodler during the first decade of the century, and a group of works in various media begun in the 1890s by the Norwegian Edvard Munch. Hodler's *Spring* (1901) (Figure 5) depicts a nude young man sitting in the right foreground, one leg drawn up, looking with a somewhat detached expression on his face in the direction of the spectator. A young woman kneels left, her expression expectant, her attitude suggesting convulsive movement. She looks at the youth, but he does not return her gaze. He remains separate from her physically, except where her foot touches his knee, and psychologically, except insofar as his look can be interpreted as one which reflects some doubt about his isolation. In *Youth Admired by Women* (1903) (Figure 6) the same youth—or, in Hodler's symbolic repertory, the same type of youth—stands right, a sparsely leafed branch in each hand, the object of admiration of a row of four women to his right, all standing with their backs to the spectator. They are, it seems, one woman seen in the act of turning to look at the youth (a common pattern in Symbolist art).[13] Nevertheless, except for the fact that the fingers of the three nearest the young man touch, the figures of the women are rendered discretely, and so is the figure of the young man. The setting is the typically sparse landscape of Hodler's symbolic work—an imaginary landscape. Like the youth in *Spring,* the youth in this painting makes no visual contact with the women looking at him, but instead looks resolutely forward, in the direction of the spectator, carrying two long-stemmed flowers that faintly suggest *thyrsi,* holding them in the stylized manner in which Bacchus sometimes carried his. In *Distant View* (Figure 7), done three years later, the same type stands on a rock with his hands against his breast, his back to a sea shrouded in mist and dotted with rocky forms. In comparison with the figure in both of the previous paintings, he looks joyful— fulfilled or near fulfillment, anticipating his immersion in the water or emerging from the water after having been immersed. In the composition of the painting, and also in its symbolic scheme, the water takes the place of the women in *Spring* and *Youth Admired by Women.* The suggestion is clearly that the youth will experience or has experienced regeneration by immersion in the water, just as the suggestion of the first two paintings is that he will experience it with the women or the girl, if he is willing.

In the work of Munch of the 1890s and the turn of the century we find the same Symbolist elements, Munch's work at the same time carrying on various Romantic traditions and looking ahead, in theme and technique, to the art of the twentieth century.[14] *Melancholy* (1901) (Figure 8) depicts a clothed young man sitting pensively by the sea, a few people in the far distance, but none in the middle distance of the beach. In *Two People* (also known as *The Lonely Ones*) (1899/ 1917) (Figure 9), the young man stands with his back to us, and so does a girl with long hair whom he would seem to be approaching. On the water, its reflection suggesting a cross, falls the light of the moon. *Withdrawal (Parting)* (1896)[15] seems to capture the moment after the meeting—a moment of rejection, but on whose part it is difficult to say. Here the long hair of the girl (now seen in profile) falls over the shoulder of the distraught-looking young man, who is turning away from her.

Other works by Munch offer similar subjects. In *Lovers in the Waves* (1896)[16] a young woman and man seem to float in the envelope of the sea. In *Attraction* (1896)[17] they gaze at each other solemnly, with the sea in the background. In *Starry Night* (ca. 1893)[18] the shore—the same as in the background in *Attraction*—is completely bare. The setting—so important to the emotional content of Romantic scenes from which these ultimately derive—alone invites the spectator to experience the renewal of the imagination offered by contact with the sea.[19]

The associations conveyed by water in Joyce's work are many and varied, from the symbol of escape from the dreaded provincialism of Ireland in *Dubliners* to the symbol of all life in *Finnegans Wake*. In *A Portrait*, which comes aesthetically and chronologically between those works, water—at the end of chapter IV at least—suggests escape and renewal: "On and on and on he strode"—this after Stephen sees the wading girl—"far out over the sands, singing wildly to the sea, crying to greet the advent of the life that had cried to him" (*P* 172). It is the sea as much as the girl in the familiar scene that has spoken to him—or, to be more precise, it is the sea through the girl. When Stephen first sees her, he sees her in the attitude of a contemplative figure by a body of water—a female version of the male types discussed previously. He watches her as she watches the sea: "A girl stood before him in midstream, alone and still, gazing out to sea" (*P* 171). Their eyes meet, but only after he has studied her for some time. The contact is broken when she withdraws her gaze to return it to the stream. In that wordless moment it is the stream that serves to speak for them both: "The first faint noise of gently moving water broke the silence, low and faint and whispering, faint as the bells of sleep; hither and thither, hither and thither: and a faint flame trembled on her cheek."

Like the youth in Hodler's *Distant View*, Stephen feels a pulsation of life in his body in response to the pulsation of the sea, the pulsation of all life. But like the youths in *Spring* and *Youth Admired by Women*—like the youth of the *fin-de-siècle* he in so many ways is—his response to this pulsation and to the wild angel who conveys it is rejection, though rejection of a special sort: he lies down till it passes, to "still the riot of his blood." For him, as for the young man of the first of Maillol's illustrations to Vergil, or the sleeping figures in the work of Vuillard that relates to this theme (see *In Bed*, Figure 1), his response is retreat:

> He closed his eyes in the languor of sleep. His eyelids trembled as if they felt the vast cyclic movement of the earth and her watchers, trembled as if they felt the strange light of some new world. His soul was swooning into some new world, fantastic, dim, uncertain as under sea, traversed by cloudy shapes and beings. A world, a glimmer, or a flower? Glimmering and trembling, trembling and unfolding, a breaking light, an opening flower, it spread in endless succession to itself. (*P* 172)

Like another youth in the art of the period—the youth in Max Klinger's *The Philosopher* (1910) (Figure 10), who reaches out to touch his own image in the mirror between which and himself lies the disproportionately large figure of a nude woman—Stephen is still not capable of making the transition from imagination to reality, from art to life, and then (to become the artist he would like to be) back again. He fails in the end to go beyond himself.

Stephen shares with the youth in *The Philosopher* a quality of self-sufficiency pushed to the extreme of solipsism, a quality shared also, as William York Tindall has pointed out at length,[20] by the young man of the *Chamber Music* sequence, who in so many ways anticipates the Stephen of the later fiction—that young man who also wanders by a body of water in search of life, "Pale flowers on his mantle, / Dark leaves on his hair" (I)—and also, of course, by Gabriel Conroy and James Duffy.

The Shelleyan young man of *Chamber Music* has found no "soul to fellow his"; he stands "Among his foes in scorn and wrath / Holding to ancient nobleness" (XXI). Like Axel in the play of Villiers de l'Isle Adam, who retreats from the world of experience to the world of the imagination, taking as his companion his love Sara, the young man of *Chamber Music*, though without a companion, has his love: "That high unconsortable one— / His love is his companion." As Tindall points out, there is the possibility of ambiguity here, "love" referring perhaps to self-love;[21] but the real ambiguity, as poems I through III indicate, for instance, is of purpose: the young man desiring at once isolation and integration, seeking the former to achieve the latter. Gabriel Conroy of "The Dead" also desires to be one with others and at the same time desires to remain apart. In a scene which resembles that of Mann's Tonio Kröger before the window, Gabriel hesitates before entering the drawing-room where the other guests are dancing and, having just failed in his attempt to be pleasant to Lily the maid, imagines how they might receive his speech:

> He waited outside the drawing-room until the waltz should finish, listening to the skirts that swept against it and to the shuffling feet.... He ... took from his waistcoat pocket a little paper and glanced at the headings he had made for his speech. He was undecided about the lines from Robert Browning, for he feared they would be above the heads of his hearers. Some quotation that they would recognize from Shakespeare or from the Melodies would be better. The indelicate clacking of the men's heels and the shuffling of their soles reminded him that their grade of culture differed from his. He would only make himself ridiculous by quoting poetry to them which they could not understand. They would think that he was airing his superior education. He would fail with them just as he had failed with the girl in the pantry. (*D* 179)

In "A Painful Case," in keeping with the tragic curve of that story, Mr. Duffy's awareness of his difference from others comes more painfully. Toward the end of the story, looking down on Phoenix Park after he learns of the death of Mrs. Sinico, he feels himself to be separated not only from the lovers below but from all humanity:

> When he gained the crest of Magazine Hill he halted and looked along the river towards Dublin, the lights of which burned redly and hospitably in the cold night. He looked down

the slope and, at the base, in the shadow of the wall of the Park, he saw some human figures lying. Those venal and furtive loves filled him with despair. He gnawed the rectitude of his life; he felt that he had been outcast from life's feast. One human being had seemed to love him and he had denied her life and happiness: he had sentenced her to ignominy, a death of shame. He knew that the prostrate creatures down by the wall were watching him and wished him gone. No one wanted him; he was outcast from life's feast. (*D* 117)

"The attitude which was constitutional with him was a silent self-occupied, contemptuous manner..." (*S* 146)[22]. Thus Joyce describes Stephen Hero in the first draft of *A Portrait,* capturing in the phrase, as in the later description of Stephen standing apart from a group of which Emma is the center, the quality of aloofness noted above in the two characters of *Dubliners:* "Stephen leaned against one of the stone pillars and regarded the further group. She stood in a ring of her companions, laughing and talking with them. The anger with which the new review had filled him gradually ebbed away and he chose to contemplate the spectacle which she and her companions offered him"(*S* 183). The somewhat younger Stephen Dedalus, in the second part of *A Portrait,* behaves at a party in much the same way, ending by singing a song and withdrawing into a corner of the room "to taste the joy of his loneliness:" "His silent watchful manner had grown upon him and he took little part in the games. The children, wearing the spoils of their crackers, danced and romped noisily and, though he tried to share their merriment, he felt himself a gloomy figure amid the gay cocked hats and sunbonnets" (*P* 68). Earlier in the novel, in chapter I, Stephen feels even more strongly a desire for detachment, though perhaps less consciously: "The wide playgrounds were swarming with boys. All were shouting and the prefects urged them on with strong cries. The evening air was pale and chilly and after every charge and thud of the footballers the greasy leather orb flew like a heavy bird through the grey light. He kept on the fringe of his line, out of sight of his prefect, out of the reach of the rude feet, feigning to run now and then. He felt his body small and weak amid the throng of players and his eyes were weak and watery" (*P* 8).

Two examples from *Jugend,* both by Hugo Höppener (known as Fidus), compare interestingly with the passages above, but particularly with the ones from "A Painful Case" and *A Portrait.* One work, *At the Great Gate,*[23] depicts a long-haired, fur-clad, partially naked youth, at least first cousin to the youth of the sea scenes discussed previously, kneeling before a high fence or grating behind which two equally youthful figures stand watching him—one a girl with her hands clasping the grating, with a look of pity, the other a boy with a switch or branch in one hand, with an almost cruel indifference. Like Mr. Duffy, the youth outside the fence seems to regret his exclusion from the park, though the love within would seem to be more than venal.[24] In the other work, the same youth, clad in the same way, stands outside a high fence on the other side of which naked youths and maidens are playing vigorously.[25] The German title,

The Iconography of the Earlier Work   15

Ausgeschlossen, carries the sense of disqualification from a sport, but also suggests exclusion in a more general sense, just as the game the young people play suggests more than a sport. In other work of the period the exclusion becomes more specifically sexual, and the excluded one takes on the qualities of the dreamer or the voyeur. In Munch's *Jealousy* (1895), for example, the male figure in the foreground is clearly excluded from the relationship of the pair in the background (his vision or fantasy) who clearly also represent Adam and Eve.[26]

Chief among the dreamers and voyeurs in Symbolist and Symbolist-related art are the artists themselves, so it is not surprising to find the motif of the dream or vision in artists' self-portraits, where it provides comment on the artist's image of himself. Emile Bernard, Gauguin's associate in the Pont-Aven group, in a self-portrait of 1891 with the subtitle *Vision* (Figure 11), makes use of the device to make such a comment on himself. He is represented, from the shoulders up, in the lower right of the canvas, and behind him and above him, in their traditional place in such paintings, appear a group of quasimythological figures, all nude, part of the vision. In the top center of this group occurs a head which clearly resembles that of the artist, on its martyred brow a crown of thorns. The familiar theme of the *poète maudit* is here linked with Christian iconography. The artist as martyr is also suggested, though more subtly, in a self-portrait by another member of the Pont-Aven group, Meyer de Haan (1890) (Figure 12) in which an architectural detail—two crossed strips of wood, separating panes of glass and coming together behind the artist's head—suggest saintliness and martyrdom. In *"Les Misérables,"* a self-portrait of 1888,[27] Gauguin suggests the same theme by reference to the popular novel of Hugo. In another work of the late 1880s, he renders this theme of artistic martyrdom as explicitly as it can be rendered. In *Christ in Gethsemane* (1889),[28] he gives the Biblical scene a provincial setting and makes the figure of Christ in the image of himself. The image of artist as martyr here not only suggests Christ; it is Christ. In another painting of the same year, *Self-Portrait with "The Yellow Christ,"*[29] as if to underscore the ironies of such depiction, Gauguin places himself before another Christ painting of 1889, *The Yellow Christ* (seen on the wall behind him, in reverse), based, as John Rewald shows, upon a primitive wooden Christ from Brittany, the face of which bears some resemblance to that of the artist.[30] Which is the face of the artist?—that is the question which the painting seems to pose.

In *A Portrait,* Stephen does not assume the face of Christ, but Christ, or the story of Christ, at least, provides a reference point by which his progress toward liberation may be measured. Chester G. Anderson has demonstrated by what means Joyce provides this reference point; it ranks, as he indicates, with artist as God and artist as hero as a motif in the work.[31]

16 The Iconography of the Earlier Work

Another familiar theme in representations of artists of this period—artist as necromancer—occurs in the very first version of *A Portrait*, which Joyce submitted to W.K. Magee of *Dana* in 1904:

> Like an alchemist he bent upon his handiwork, bringing together the mysterious elements, separating the subtle from the gross. For the artist the rhythms of phrase and period, the symbols of word and allusion, were paramount things. And was it any wonder that out of this marvellous life, wherein he had annihilated and rebuilt experience, laboured and despaired, he came forth at last with a single purpose—to reunite the children of the spirit, jealous and long-divided, to reunite them against fraud and principality.[32]

This passage anticipates Stephen's description, in *A Portrait*, of the artist as a priest of the imagination. It also compares interestingly with Paul Sérusier's *Portrait of Paul Ranson in Nabi Garb* (1890),[33] and with Gauguin's satiric Symbolist self-portrait with halo,[34] both of which reflect the view, prevalent in the 1890s, of the artist-seer.

If Joyce, by the time he wrote *A Portrait*, largely rejected the Symbolist view of the artist, he did not reject it *in toto*. Stephen's definition of the artist—"The artist, like the God of the creation, remains within or behind or beyond or above his handiwork, invisible, refined out of existence, indifferent, paring his fingernails" (*P* 215)—not only corresponds in many ways to the attitude of Joyce himself, but also the to the practice of many Symbolist painters in their subtler renderings of themselves and their peers. In some instances these renderings are merely variations on representations of the artist common from the time of the Renaissance; in others, however, they point ahead to the even subtler artistic presences of Cubist work of the period after 1910. They testify to the importance in Symbolist art of the doctrine in Symbolist poetry, enunciated by Mallarmé in "Crise de vers," that the artist must become "impersonalized," must disappear into the work.[35]

Gauguin, in his 1889 portrait of the painter Emile Schuffenecker and his family, shows the painter not in the act of painting, but to one side, as if contemplating his subject—his wife and children.[36] Schuffenecker's position in this painting corresponds to Gauguin's placement of himself in other works of the late 1880s and 1890s which, though not self-portraits, are illustrative of the Symbolist view of the artist and his work—a view shared by Joyce. In *Te Po (The Great Night)*, a woodcut from his first voyage to Tahiti, in which the figure of a dying girl lies stretched at length in the center of the picture (1894) (Figure 13), Gauguin puts his own figure in the small group of spirits looking on, the first figure (seen only shoulders and above) to the right of center. In this case the artist is also in a sense contemplating his subject, but an even subtler relationship between artist and subject, or center of interest, is suggested: Gauguin is not invisible, but he is certainly well-disguised, and if his presence at all shapes our interpretation of the scene, it does so by a denial of its own importance. We recognize him, but we also recognize, by his effort to conceal himself, a comment on the role of the artist in relationship to his work. The work is impersonal, and must be judged impersonally. Such is the whole tendency of Gauguin's Symbolism—to strip away inessential details in order to to produce work in which color and line combine to produce an effect in themselves, an impersonal, largely nonliterary and, when fully successful, universal aesthetic effect.[37]

In the earlier and better-known *Vision after the Sermon* (1888), Jacob wrestles with the angel as a group of Breton peasants, their backs to us, look on. At the right of this group, Gauguin again appears to have put himself, head bowed, as if meditating on the scene he has created.[38] The link between this *Vision* and the vision of Bernard (Figure 11) is obvious, with the figure of the artist below and the vision above; the difference is that here the artist is not looking in the direction of the spectator, inviting him to perceive the vision as an outgrowth of the artist's imagination, but away from him, towards the ground. The invitation is less direct; the emphasis more on the scene imagined than on the imaginer. The *Still Life with Japanese Print* of the following year (1889) provides an example of another kind of disguise, for here, in partial payment of his debt to the Japanese masters, Gauguin puts himself, in the form of a ceramic self-portrait vase which he had done shortly before the painting, in front of a vase of flowers, with a Japanese print on the wall in the background.[39] In one of his illustrations to Wilde's *Salomé*, Aubrey Beardsley, with similar results, wittily makes over the moon in the image of Wilde, who then contemplates a scene of the play he has created. In this case, however, the artist (or playwright) is neither completely invisible, as Stephen would have him, nor even too much disguised.[40]

Munch, in an early version of a recurring subject in his *oeuvre,* puts his own figure in a less detached but slightly disguised relationship to others in *Death in the Sickroom* (1895) (Figure 14). Here the figure of Munch—his head turned so that we can see only one side of his face and the back of his head—serves to unite the group of figures in the foreground with the group nearer the deathbed in the background.[41] He makes of himself a subtle connecting force in the composition, as Joyce makes of the author a subtle guiding force in the narrative of *Dubliners* and *A Portrait*. The ceramic figure of Gauguin does nearly the same thing in the *Still Life* discussed above, connecting the treatment of line and color in the print with the treatment of the same elements in the vase at left.

This line of inquiry takes us beyond similarities of imagery in Joyce's work and the art of Symbolism into similarities of technique. Having noted the many similarities between Joyce's representation of Stephen and related types and the representation of the artist in the art of the 1890s and the turn of the century, it is necessary to note only one more, of key importance to *A Portrait* and to Stephen's definition of himself there, as well as to the definition of the artist in Western civilization from the time of the Renaissance onward. I refer of course to the artist as hero, a theme by no means absent from the art of Symbolism, as, for example, Klinger's well-known representation of Beethoven attests.[42] As Stephen, at the end of *A Portrait*, goes to encounter "the reality of experience" and forge in his soul "the uncreated conscience" of his race, he thinks not of bird-girls or of malignant creatures and horrible visions but of:

> The spell of arms and voices: the white arms of roads, their promise of close embraces and the black arms of tall ships that stand against the moon, their tale of distant nations. They are held out to say: We are alone. Come. And the voices say with them: we are your kinsmen. And the air is thick with their company as they call to me, their kinsman, making ready to go, shaking the wings of their exultant and terrible youth. (*P* 252)

In Rudolph Jettmar's *The Poet* (Figure 15), a young man sits up in bed in a darkened room, a reflective expression on his face; in the upper part of the work, the same young man appears, winged, in a heroic posture and mythological setting, bodies behind him and strewn about his feet. Though perhaps more Nietzschean than Vergilian, Jettmar's etching, like Stephen's dream, provides a quintessential representation of the heroic conception of the artist.[43]

The Girl with Long Flowing Hair

> Hair: the mind turning again to this without adverting to its colour, adverting only to a distinctive sexual mark and to its growth and mystery.... The softly growing symbol of her girlhood.... Ivy and roses: she gathered ivy often when out in the evening with girls. Roses grew then a sudden scarlet note in the memory which may be a dim suggestion of the roses of the body. The ivy and the roses carry on and up, out of the idea of growth, through a creeping vegetable life into ardent perfumed flower life the symbol of mysteriously growing girlhood, her hair. (*E* 119-120).[44]

In these terms Joyce, in the notes to *Exiles*, describes Bertha's thoughts about her hair, which becomes, with the vegetable life and perfumed flowers it grows into, a symbol of "growing girlhood." These notes not only anticipate the description of Molly's hair in the final episode of *Ulysses*, they also recall the girl who appears in Joyce's early poems—the "Goldenhair" of *Chamber Music*—and repeat in their emphasis upon long flowing hair a descriptive detail which characterizes the girls or women of more than one intervening work, in particular the bird-girl of chapter IV of *A Portrait*. They also parallel precisely the image of the girl with long flowing hair, from which leaves and flowers grow, popular in the visual arts of the 1890s and the turn of the century.

Joyce himself points to the connection with *Chamber Music* when, shifting into the author's voice, he writes in the notes to *Exiles*:

Ribbon for her hair. Its fitting ornament for the eyes of others, and lastly for his eyes. Girlhood becomes virginity and puts on "the snood that is the sign of maidenhood." A proud and shy instinct turns her mind away from the loosening of her bound-up hair—however sweet or longed for or inevitable—and she embraces that which is hers alone and not hers and his also—happy distant dancing days, distant, gone forever, dead, or killed? (*E* 120)

The phrase "the snood that is the sign of maidenhood" comes, of course, from *Chamber Music* XI, which deals with a similar theme:

> Bid adieu, adieu, adieu,
>   Bid adieu to girlish days,
> Happy Love is come to woo
>   Thee and woo thy girlish ways—
> The zone that doth become thee fair,
> The snood upon thy yellow hair.
>
> When thou hast heard his name upon
>   The bugles of the cherubim
> Begin thou softly to unzone
>   Thy girlish bosom unto him
> And softly to undo the snood
> That is the sign of maidenhood.

The play is at least partly the account of Bertha's leaving behind girlish days for adult complications—of her being forced into the moral world of adults by Richard's contrivance. Like Gretta Conroy in "The Dead," Bertha would prefer "happy distant dancing days" to the reality she is proffered. Unlike the snood of the girl in *Chamber Music* XI, the snood Bertha must undo is more spiritual than physical. "The soul like the body may have a virginity," Joyce observes elsewhere in the notes to *Exiles* (*E* 113). "For the woman to yield it or for the man to take it is the act of love"—for which, like the girl of *Chamber Music*, Bertha must let down her hair.

Other poems of the *Chamber Music* sequence also refer to hair tumbling down: "Thy kiss descending / Sweeter were / With a soft tumult / Of thy hair" (XX); or blowing in the wind: "Oread let thy laughter run / Till the irreverent mountain air / Ripple all thy flying hair" (XXV); or being combed: "Silently she's combing, / Combing her long hair" (XXIV). And in V, giving her a name, the speaker implores: "Lean out of the window / Goldenhair." With the exception of the eyes, no other feature of the girl receives so much attention.

Not only in *Chamber Music* but also elsewhere in the early work the same detail recurs. In the first version of *A Portrait*, the "Portrait of the Artist" written in 1904, in a passage which anticipates the end of chapter IV of the later work, the wading girl makes her first appearance, only in the plural. The hair of these girls is the first feature to be remarked: "Wandering over the arid, grassy hills or along the strand, avowedly in quest of shellfish, he had grown almost impatient of the day. Waders, into whose childish or girlish hair, girlish or childish dresses, the very wilfulness of the sea had entered—even they had not fascinated."[45] In "Araby," in *Dubliners,* the narrator describes Mangan's sister in the following terms: "She was waiting for us, her figure defined by the light from the half-opened door.... Her dress swung as she moved her body and the soft rope of her hair tossed from side to side" (*D* 30). In "The Dead," when Gabriel imagines the attitude in which he would paint Gretta standing on the stairs, he thinks of a way to bring out the color of her hair: "Her blue felt hat would show off the bronze of her hair against the darkness and the dark panels of her skirt would show off the light ones" (*D* 210).[46] Later, in recollection of a few days before, Gabriel thinks, "... the flame of the gas lit up the rich bronze of her hair, which he had seen drying at the fire a few days before" (*D* 212). In the poetry other than *Chamber Music* the same detail is cited in "Tutto è sciolto"—"The clear young eyes' soft look, the candid brow, / The fragrant hair, / Falling as through the silence falleth now / Dusk of the air."[47]

In *A Portrait,* Eileen, Stephen's childhood sweetheart, is described in part: "Her fair hair had streamed out behind her like gold in the sun" (*P* 43). In chapter III of the novel, Stephen imagines the Day of Judgment, when "his sins, the jeweleyed harlots of his imagination, fled before the hurricane, squeaking like mice in their terror and huddled under a mane of hair" (*P* 115), a figure which recalls the whores at the beginning of that section, "coming out of their houses making ready for the night, yawning lazily after their sleep and settling the hairpins in their clusters of hair" (*P* 102), and the girls, no longer so appealing, toward the end: "Frowsy girls sat along the curbstones before their baskets. Their dank hair hung trailed over their brows" (*P* 140). The hair of the girl Davin encounters in the hills is "hanging," as he puts it in his colloquial account: "She was half undressed as if she was going to bed when I knocked and she had her hair hanging" (*P* 182). The girl Stephen encounters on the beach has hair long and girlish: "... her long fair hair was girlish: and girlish, and touched with the wonder of mortal beauty, her face" (*P* 171).

The artists of Art Nouveau placed a similar emphasis upon long flowing hair, which, however—like Bertha's in the notes to *Exiles*—typically became entwined with, or grew into, leaves and flowers, suggesting the traditional relationship between women and fecundity. In a printed velvet design by the Belgian illustrator and designer Alphonse Mucha (ca. 1900) (Figure 16), the hair of the woman is entwined with the branches and leaves of a vine or tree to the extent that the two become virtually inseparable. If there are no roses, as in Joyce's notes, carrying on and up the idea of growth contained in the flowing hair, there is at any rate "a creeping vegetable life" in clear relationship to the mysterious symbol of the hair. A brooch design (ca. 1899-1902) by Paul Albert Beaudoin, illustrates, in gold and enamel, with pearls and brilliants, the great variety of decorative forms in which the girl of Art Nouveau appeared. Here, in an ornate piece of jewelry, her face is surrounded by a few violets and their leaves, these seeming to grow out of her long hair.[48] Ubiquitous as well as abundant, the girl occurred in places other than France and Belgium, in other genres and forms. An initial from the same period by Kolomon Moser, who was part of the Jugendstil movement in Vienna, depicts the same type, the letter "S" superimposed on her profile, flowers in her hair.[49] A woodcut by Fred Hyland for *The Savoy* shows the girl, with the same characteristic features, as represented in 1896 in England.[50] Even earlier than the 1890s, Heywood Sumner, in his design for the binding of an English edition of Friedrich de la Motte-Fouqué's *Undine* (1888), uses the same type of figure, her hair blending into vines and forming the border of the design.[51] Robert Burns, in an illustration done in 1891 and published four years later in the first volume of the Scottish publication *Evergreen* (Figure 17), makes of the long-haired girl a symbol of a different sort of fecundity, not vegetable, but animal. This long-haired girl is closer in expressive force to the girl of Art Nouveau: nude and seen from the back, she is surrounded by a swirl of birds and fishes.

The Pre-Raphaelite woman has also long, flowing hair. Indeed, it is largely from the Pre-Raphaelites, in particular from Rossetti, that this feature of the ideal woman in the work of the Symbolists and the artists of Art Nouveau comes. She also typically has prominent eyes, which stare intently at the spectator, providing an imaginative link between the image on the canvas and the viewer of that image. As Wilde remarks in the Preface to *The Picture of Dorian Gray*, "It is the spectator, and not life, that art really mirrors." In discussing an early story by Rossetti, John Dixon Hunt observes that, to the first spectator of the image of the woman—the artist who creates it—she "appears as a visible embodiment of his soul" and, furthermore, "that the artist should honour his soul, which means painting the images of his soul, the various moods of a beautiful woman."[52] In a study for *Astarte Syriaca* (Figure 18) the tresses are flowing, and the gaze is typically penetrating. In *La Pia de'Tolomei*, in which the pensiveness of the earlier images has given way to the dolorousness which marks the later Rossetti women, the tresses flow directly in front of, and become virtually entwined with, the ivy on the wall, much in the manner of Art Nouveau, where hair and vine become one. In this case, the gaze of the woman is directed somewhere far behind, and below, the left shoulder of the spectator.[53]

In Joyce's work the feature which receives most attention, next to that of the hair, is the eyes. In *Dubliners*, Mr. Duffy, an artist to the extent that he conforms to certain norms of behavior of the *poète maudit*, is particularly struck by the eyes of Mrs. Sinico:

> Her face, which must have been handsome, had remained intelligent. It was an oval face with strongly marked features. The eyes were very dark blue and steady. Their gaze began with a defiant note but was confused by what seemed a deliberate swoon of the pupil into the iris,

revealing for an instant a temperament of great sensibility. The pupil reasserted itself quickly, this half-disclosed nature fell again under the reign of prudence, and her astrakhan jacket, moulding a bosom of a certain fulness, struck the note of defiance more definitely. (*D* 109-110)

Even more striking, in terms of the Rossetti ideal, is the manner in which Mr. Duffy sees himself, somewhat later in the story, in her eyes: "He thought that in her eyes he would ascend to an angelical stature; and, as he attached the fervent nature of his companion more closely to him, he heard the strange impersonal voice which he recognised as his own, insisting on the soul's incurable loneliness. We cannot give ourselves, it said: we are our own" (*D* 111). In the sense that Mrs. Sinico remains a projection of certain qualities of Mr. Duffy's, their relationship cannot develop; more precisely, Mr. Duffy sees in Mrs. Sinco an aspect of himself which he does not wish to acknowledge—his "fervent nature," which he wishes to be subservient to his spiritual nature, "an angelical stature." In the same sense, Stephen, at the end of chapter IV of *A Portrait*, does not wish to acknowledge, in the eyes of the wading girl, as in her whole being, an aspect of himself which he wishes to remain buried: "... her eyes turned to him in quiet sufferance of his gaze, without shame or wantonness" (*P* 171). Like Mrs. Sinico, the wading girl is in a sense a projection of all Stephen desires, and rejects. In these instances, as elsewhere—"Through the clear mirror of your eyes, / Through the soft sigh of kiss to kiss, / Desolate winds assail with cries / The shadowy garden where love is" (*Chamber Music* XXIX); "There was something striking in her appearance.... Farrington gazed admiringly at the plump arm which she moved very often and with much grace; and when, after a little time, she answered his gaze he admired still more her large dark brown eyes. The oblique staring expression in them fascinated him" ("Counterparts," *D* 95)—the use of the image of the eyes, the *reading* of the eyes, is at least half-ironic, since in nearly every instance the male figure clearly does not wish to acknowledge (or, in the case of Farrington, because of lack of money, is unable to acknowledge) what he sees of himself in the woman's eyes. "We have all seen in our own day in England," Wilde observes in "The Decay of Lying," "how a certain curious and fascinating type of beauty ... has so influenced Life that whenever one goes to a private view or to an artistic salon one sees ... the mystic eyes of Rossetti's dream, the long ivory throat, the strange square-cut jaw, the loosened shadowy hair that he so ardently loved...."[54] When the characters of Joyce see this beauty, they are ultimately reluctant to acknowledge what they see.

The mixture of the spiritual and the physical, the cerebral and the sensuous, in the Pre-Raphaelite woman reflects the changing moods of the spectator, but these contrasting qualities of the woman are scarcely distinguishable from one another. John Dixon Hunt remarks of Rossetti's work,

It has sometimes been the fashion to see in his work a divided impulse which makes him "thrill to the appeal both of Mary Virgin and of Mary Magdalene, of Beatrice and of Jenny, of the Blessed Damozel and of Circe." What is important in this emphasis is that each of these two types serves as some different symbol in his work; but neither does he wish to maintain any strict distinctions between sensualist and idealist notions...."[55]

The same distinctions are blurred in another, later version of ideal woman, related to, if not derived from, the Pre-Raphaelite—the girl of Symbolist art. Ideally, the Symbolist girl, as George Mauner notes in describing the Nabi rendition of her, was "of interest not anatomically, but rather as a vessel of the spirit...."[56] Her purpose was to inspire contemplation, a state of meditation; she was not so much, like the Pre-Raphaelite woman, to reflect the moods of the spectator, but to lead the spectator beyond moods, beyond temperament, to the universal Idea. The spectator before the canvas on which the Pre-Raphaelite woman appears, whether he is an artist or not, sees himself in her staring eyes; the spectator before the canvas on which the Symbolist girl appears, her eyes typically closed, sees himself in her attitude. The Symbolist manner is less direct than the Pre-Raphaelite, just as the meditative state it suggests is less active than the state suggested by Pre-Raphaelite art typically is. Ideally, Symbolist art is static, the visual equivalent of the silence in Symbolist drama, in which all things happen. Thus in *Closed Eyes* (1890) (Figure 19) by Odilon Redon, the head of the woman is slightly inclined and her eyes closed. She is caught in the Symbolist moment of repose. In a later Redon, the *Silence* (ca. 1911), her eyes are half-closed and, in the slightest of gestures, she raises two fingers to her lips.[57] The Nabi painters frequently represent the woman or girl with her back turned, or standing at an angle, the obliqueness of which prevents eye contact of the sort the Pre-Raphaelites sought to create. K.-X. Roussel's *Maiden on the Path* (1890) places the girl, seen from behind, to one side of the canvas, a road curving up a hillside to her left. Her hair is bound up at the back of her neck, but she is obviously the slender, long-haired vessel of the spirit to be seen in other Nabi work, and her projected journey is one of the spirit or the imagination. The French *vierge* conveys an additional spiritual sense to the title, since it also means "virgin."[58] In the same spirit, the Nabi Maurice Denis's illustration to "The Blessed Damozel" provides an interesting contrast to the ideal woman of the Rossetti poem. In the poem, "The blessed damozel leaned out / From the gold bar of Heaven; / Her eyes were deeper than the depth / Of waters stilled at even...."[59] Denis chooses not to represent the eyes at all, but gives us a Symbolist version of the Pre-Raphaelite girl, in profile, her eyes cast downward.[60] No girl in Joyce's early work precisely parallels this type in the visual arts of the period, but one at least comes close.

However much these girls are designed ideally to provoke the meditative state, they frequently provoke something else as well. Child-women—in Mauner's phrase "pale, slight, withdrawn"—they are often more erotic than static. In the work of Maeterlinck, which provided the literary prototype of the girl for the Nabis, Mélisande (1892) and the Princesse Maleine (1889) show traces of this erotic quality; so, too, does the young woman the law student imagines in Édouard Dujardin's *Les Lauriers sont coupés,* which first appeared serially in 1887, who is described as having the body of a female child ("d'enfant féminin").[61] In Joyce's early work the figure that comes closest to this type of innocence and sensuality is the wading girl at the end of chapter IV of *A Portrait.*

By 1891 Pierre Quillard, in the pages of the *Mercure de France,* can speak of the *femme-enfant* as a literary type, but one, however, in whom the paradox of sensuality and innocence has become more cruel than beguiling. In reviewing a novel by Catulle Mendès entitled *La Femme-Enfant,* he writes:

> "An ambiguous creature of a spirit too vile for tenderness, with eyes too pure for debauchery," thus is defined Lillian, the latest arrival among those who sum up in themselves and exaggerate in order to become real beings in the world of art one of the multiple aspects of women. The absolute contradiction between what she is and what she appears to be, between the ingenuousness of "the dream child" and the knowledge, in theory and in action, of the most guileful obscenity, make her a monster apart, very well conceived and very perfect.[62]

In describing Polly Mooney of "The Boarding House" in *Dubliners,* Joyce emphasizes the same paradoxical quality, referring to her "wise innocence" in dealing with her mother. The phrase occurs when Mrs. Mooney discovers that Polly is pregnant, and they have their conversation about the matter:

> Both had been somewhat awkward, of course. She [Mrs. Mooney] had been made awkward by her not wishing to receive the news in too cavalier a fashion or to seem to have connived and Polly had been made awkward not merely because allusions of that kind always made her awkward but also because she did not wish it to be thought that in her wise innocence she had divined the intention behind her mother's tolerance. (*D* 64)

Polly's behavior thus carries out the description of her earlier in the story, a description which links her with both the Pre-Raphaelite woman and the Symbolist child-woman: "Polly was a slim girl of nineteen; she had light soft hair and a small full mouth. Her eyes, which were grey with a shade of green through them, had a habit of glancing upwards when she spoke with anyone, which made her look like a little perverse madonna" (*D* 62-63).

Besides suggesting the Pre-Raphaelite woman and the Symbolist child-woman, this description of Polly also suggests the more sensuous *Madonna* of Edvard Munch (Figure 20), one of the most celebrated images of woman in art of this period, in which the concept of the miraculous conception gives way to that of biological determinism, with a heavy-lidded, long-haired Madonna (not a *femme-enfant*, but a slightly older, more experienced type) occupying the center of the picture and spermatozoa forming the frame, with a foetus grotesquely occupying the lower left hand corner. Munch himself linked his *Madonna* with death as well as life, describing a version of her in these terms: "The pause when the entire world halted in its orbit. Your face embodies all the world's beauty. Your lips, crimson red like the coming fruit, slide apart as in pain. The smile of a corpse. Now life and death join hands. The chain is joined that ties the thousands of past generations to the thousands of generations to come."[63] This symbolism brings to mind Joyce's later treatment of Molly Bloom or Anna Livia Plurabelle; for the wisely innocent Polly, a more telling comparison may be provided by various versions of Eve.

In a Gauguin work of 1889 Eve, the traditional figure of woman willfully misguiding man, and of woman willfully misguided, takes on certain trappings of *la femme-enfant*. Young, girlish, with long hair—the serpent on the tree behind her—she appears as a peasant girl in the *Breton Eve* (Figure 21). The same figure appears in the background of Gauguin's satanic portrait of Meyer de Haan, done in the same year in Brittany, but whether as a vision of tempted or tempter it is difficult to say.[64] Munch's Eve is girlish and long-haired in the background vision of the *Jealousy* discussed above. Related work also occurs in the pages of *Die Jugend*, for instance Rudolf Riemerschmied's *Eve and the Serpent*, in which a long-haired Eve is seen in a summer setting, kneeling by a tree, with the serpent nearby in the grass.[65] The same figure appears, in Riemerschmied's *Summer Day*, beside a pond, combing or binding her long hair.[66] To the extent that she is too wise to be innocent, and brings to his fall an innocent man, Polly can be identified with the Eve of tradition. To the extent that she is childlike in her beauty, she can be identified with the Eve of the painting of the 1890s.

But if Polly's problem is traditional, it is also hereditary. Polly, whose innocence was surrendered as a condition of her birth, and in whose eyes fresh green makes little headway against prevailing grey, cannot go beyond her mothering or herself. In the art of the 1890s, narcissism is a frequent theme, and so it is in "The Boarding-House" and elsewhere in early Joyce. In "The Boarding-House" and "The Dead" it is symbolized by preoccupation with one's image in a mirror. At the end of the story, as Bob Moran goes downstairs to meet with Mrs. Mooney and render her the only answer he can, Polly regains her composure quickly by self-inspection: "Polly sat for a little time on the side of the bed, crying. Then she dried her eyes and went over to the looking-glass. She dipped the end of the towel in the water-jug and refreshed her eyes with the cool water. She looked at herself in profile and readjusted a hairpin above her ear. Then she went back to the bed again and sat at the foot" (*D* 68). Earlier in the story, Polly's mother, no less a prisoner in the cell of herself, surveys her image in a mirror: "She stood up and surveyed herself in the pier-glass. The decisive expression of her great florid face satisfied her..." (*D* 65). Maria, in "Clay," also inspects herself before paying a visit to her brother: "... she took off her working skirt and her house-boots and laid her best skirt out on the bed and her tiny dress-boots beside the foot of the bed. She changed her blouse too and, as she stood before the mirror, she thought of how she used to dress for mass on Sunday morning when she was a young girl; and she looked with quaint affection at the diminutive body which she had so often adorned. In spite of its years she found it a nice tidy little body" (*D* 101).[67]

In a cover drawing for the third volume of *The Yellow Book,* Beardsley joins in this narcissistic theme, depicting a corrupt woman before a mirror, her lips pursed, a powder puff in her hand. In keeping with the tendency of Art Nouveau, though with more wit than one usually finds there, he has here reduced the whole theme to a vignette.[68] In the symbolic scheme of certain works—in keeping with the ultimate source of the image in the Narcissus legend—water is substituted for glass.[69] (Compare Polly Mooney's first refreshing her eyes with cool water and then gazing at her countenance in the mirror.) In Aman-Jean's *The Mirror,* a young woman, breasts uncovered to view, bends over a basin of water to study her reflection, the setting a garden.[70] In the lithograph *Le Bouquet matinal, les larmes (Morning Bouquet, Tears),*[71] from the album *Amour (1911),* Maurice Denis subtly juxtaposes the image of a pensive woman holding a bouquet with the image of a small pond in the middle distance. These scenes and others like them suggest the affinity between treatments of the theme of narcissism with male and female protagonists: though the sex of the subjects may differ, the terms of symbolic representation remain the same.

As temptress Polly has some little success, but her brand of tempting is not the only one encountered—or sought—in the pages of early Joyce. Some are even more direct, and set forth in more blatant images. In poem XX of *Chamber Music* the woman becomes—in the imagination of the speaker, at least—the more aggressive one: "Thy kiss descending / Sweeter were / With a soft tumult / Of thy hair"; and in the later poem, "A Prayer," she becomes a kind of vampire: "Draw from me still / My slow life! Bend deeper on me, threatening head, / Proud by my downfall, remembering, pitying / Him who is, him who was!"[72] A color woodcut of 1896 by Munch depicts a man's head enwreathed by the hair of a woman, who is looking down at him lovingly, or perhaps possessively (Figure 22). This work compares symbolically with the violent *Vampire* of the same period (1894), in which the woman's hair trails over the man's, and her lips are sealed to the back of his neck.[73]

Of two other popular types of feminine evil of the 1890s—the Sphinx and Salomé—the temptress of the villanelle in *A Portrait* suggests the former. Possibly the most celebrated literary rendition of the Sphinx was Wilde's, and a comparison between the creature imagined by the young student of his poem

(1894) and the creature imagined by Stephen in *A Portrait* is revealing of the latter. The setting of Wilde's poem is the student's room, where, in a corner, "for longer than my fancy thinks / A beautiful and silent Sphinx has watched me through the shifting gloom" (142).[74] The Sphinx combines the qualities of woman and animal, becoming an eternal image—and in a strange way an ideal—of all that is grotesque and depraved: "Come forth, my lovely seneschal! / so somnolent, so statuesque! / Come forth, you exquisite grotesque! / half woman and half animal!" (143). Among the lovers the speaker imagines for this exquisite grotesque, before settling on Ammon, is "the god of the Assyrian / Whose wings, like strange transparent talc, rose high above his hawk-faced head" (146). After imagining the fate of Ammon in the clutches of the Sphinx, the speaker ends by banishing her from his thoughts, and his room: "Get hence, you loathsome mystery! / Hideous animal, get hence! / You wake in me each bestial sense, / You make me what I would not be" (151). He concludes first with a reference to his religious creed, and then with the image of the crucifix, traditional protection against mysteries of all sorts: "You make my creed a barren sham, you wake foul dreams of sensual life" (152); and then, "Go thou before, and leave me to my crucifix"—"Whose pallid burden, sick with pain, / watches the world with wearied eyes, / And keeps for every soul that dies, / and weeps for every soul in vain" (152).[75]

In *A Portrait*, Stephen first concentrates on the image of the temptress: "Conscious of his desire she was waking from odorous sleep, the temptress of his villanelle. Her eyes, dark and with a look of languor, were opening to his eyes. Her nakedness yielded to him, radiant, warm, odorous and lavish-limbed, enfolded him like a shining cloud, enfolded him like water with a liquid life" (*P* 223). As the student of Wilde's poem imagines the centuries' worship of the creature of his imagination, so the speaker in Stephen's villanelle imagines an offering to the idol: "*... sacrificing hands upraise / The chalice flowing to the brim.*" The question repeated throughout the poem is in essence the question raised by the speaker in the poem by Wilde—"*Are you not weary of ardent ways?*"—and the answer, implicit in another line repeated, is the same: "*Tell no more of enchanted days.*" Like the speaker in his villanelle, Stephen rejects the demands of the flesh and of life, and in the section which follows the composition of the villanelle envisions his escape by flight from the net which has nearly ensnared him. Then, fearful yet desirous of escape, he imagines Thoth, "god of writers": "A sense of fear of the unknown moved in the heart of his weariness, a fear of symbols and portents, of the hawklike man whose name he bore soaring out of his captivity on osierwoven wings, of Thoth, the god of writers, writing with a reed upon a tablet and bearing on his narrow ibis head the cusped moon" (*P* 225). If the speaker of Wilde's poem hopes to escape what he considers bestiality by way of the religion of Christ, Stephen hopes to escape similar snares by way of the religion of art, but for Stephen the escape remains an illusion, since it is only by acceptance of his sensual nature that he will become an artist. In no sense indebted to Wilde's poem, the section of *A Portrait* examined here treats a similar theme with a similar situation and set of characters (note that the speaker of the poem is a young man of scarcely twenty, in contrast with the "thousand weary centuries" of the Sphinx). The irony of Joyce's use of this situation and theme, as in his use of the theme of the *poète maudit* in developing Stephen's character, is all the more apparent in comparison with a work like Wilde's, which is much more serious about all three.

The Sphinx figure in the art of the 1890s and the turn of the century had been anticipated several decades earlier by the *Oedipus and the Sphinx* of Gustave Moreau (1864), the painter of ideas mentioned in *Ulysses*.[76] In Moreau's work the sphinx, a small winged creature with a woman's face and breasts, clings to the body of the standing Oedipus. In German art the treatment of the subject is typically more naturalistic. Franz von Stuck's *The Kiss of the Sphinx*, for example, depicts a much more sensuous creature, though she is still half-animal, bending backwards with the force of her kiss the naked figure of a man.[77] Still another version of the same subject by the same artist depicts a sphinx who is, like Stephen's temptress, all woman.[78] In a title plate for an edition of *Les Diaboliques*, Félicien Rops gives an added twist to the theme, providing a suggestion of the Eve of tradition, at any rate making the allegory of the Sphinx plainer: a naked woman clings to the neck of the sphinx, half-woman and half-animal, while in the background, on the wings of the sphinx, the figure of Satan perches.[79]

Perhaps the most prominent type of evil in the period of the 1890s and shortly before in the visual arts was the figure of Salomé, and certainly one of the most celebrated representations of this figure—besides Beardsley's, in illustration to Wilde's play—was the *Apparition* of Gustave Moreau (Figure 23).[80] Moreau, who did many versions of the subject, here shows Salomé, bejewelled and more than slightly chagrined, standing left, pointing to the head of the Baptist, which floats in the air right rear. If certain treatments of the subject, like Moreau's, set the fashion which made Wilde's play possible, others, like Beardsley's, came into being as a result of the play.

Painters and illustrators found the dance and the head on the platter the subjects most to their liking in treating Salomé. Joyce liked the image of the head well enough to use it in *A Portrait*, in reference to Cranly,[81] but what of the image of Salomé? In Joyce's early work she exists only by allusion, but she defines, however obliquely, the dance of the male figure in the twenty-third Epiphany, and the character of the dancer, a boy "lithe and serious": "His dancing is not the dancing of harlots, the dance of the daughters of Herodias. It goes up from the midst of the people, sudden and young and male, and falls again to earth in tremulous sobbing to die upon its triumph."[82] The calculated seductiveness of Salomé is the opposite of the innocent frenzy of the boy whirling before the multitude, and Joyce clearly has in mind the Salomé of the nineteenth century, not the innocent of the Middle Ages.[83]

It has frequently enough been observed that the women and girls of *A Portrait* embody contradictory themes; indeed, they would seem to function in the novel chiefly on the symbolic level, never becoming, as in *Dubliners, Stephen Hero,* or *Ulysses,* characters in their own right. To the extent that this is true, they find their parallel in the visual arts in such figures as those of Munch and others who suggest at once the erotic and the spiritual. But the best parallel—the visual arts being perhaps more limited in this respect, or less resonant—may be in such works as the Dutch Symbolist Jan Toorop's *The Three Brides,* with the nun, bride of Christ, on the left, the human bride, a virgin, in the center, and the bride of Satan on the right[84]—or Munch's *Woman* (also known as *The Sphinx* and *The Three Stages of Woman*) (Figure 24), which Munch once recalled having explained to Ibsen in these terms: "Here is the dreaming woman—there the woman hungry for life—and the woman as a nun—standing pale-faced behind the trees."[85] Munch and Toorop require three figures to express the various characteristics of the eternal feminine as they appeared to the artist of the 1890s; Joyce, with the temptress before whom priests kneel, or the wading girl, "the angel of mortal youth and beauty, an envoy from the fair courts of life," manages with one.

The Chamber and the Forest

The characters of the earlier work of Joyce achieve fictional life not only as a result of certain details of their persons, or certain qualities of their dream life, or certain aspects of their relations with others, or certain allusions they make or opinions they hold, or—most importantly in the case of Joyce—through the language in which all of these are described, but also, as we have already seen in part, as a result of the settings in which they are encountered. These settings, interior and exterior, have different effects on the characters of the earlier work, and small details of each add to the significance of the behavior we observe. The exterior settings in particular compare closely with exterior scenes in Symbolist art—with landscapes with figures and landscapes without. The interior settings in Joyce's work provide more points of contrast than of similarity with corresponding scenes in Symbolist art, but, by these points of contrast, we can perhaps grasp more fully the symbolic significance of the exterior scenes.

Nearly halfway through "The Dead," Gabriel, having ended, with Miss Ivors, his first dance of the evening and his second unpleasant encounter with a woman other than his wife, retires into the embrasure of a window and looks across the Liffey to Phoenix Park: "Gabriel's warm trembling fingers tapped the cold pane of the window. How cool it must be outside! How pleasant it would be to walk out alone, first along by the river and then through the park! The snow would be lying on the branches of the trees and forming a bright cap on the top of the Wellington monument. How much more pleasant it would be there than at the supper-table!" (*D* 192). Later in the story, as he rises from the table to begin his after-dinner speech, he thinks longingly again of the Park and of the whole world of Dublin: "People, perhaps, were standing in the snow on the quay outside, gazing up at the lighted windows and listening to the waltz music. The air was pure there. In the distance lay the park where the trees were weighted with snow" (*D* 202). These passages are linked, in the imagery of the story, with the famous final evocation, which begins with Gabriel looking out the window of the hotel room he is sharing with his wife: "A few light taps upon the pane made him turn to the window. It had begun to snow again. He watched sleepily the flakes, silver and dark, falling obliquely against the lamplight. The time had come for him to set out on his journey westward" (*D* 223). They are also linked with other passages in *Dubliners* and other earlier works in which the interior world and the exterior world, particularly in the form of forest or wood, become negative and positive polarities, the exterior setting an invitation to renewal of self which the interior denies.

In "A Painful Case," the same conjunction of sights that moves Gabriel—of the Liffey and, with lovers sprawled in its midst, Phoenix Park—leads Mr. Duffy to gnaw the rectitude of his life, to feel that "he had been outcast from life's feast" (*D* 117). In contrast with the sense of life in this scene, his room, as described at the beginning of the story, is monastic and forbidding:

> The lofty walls of his uncarpeted room were free from pictures. He had himself bought every article of furniture in the room: a black iron bedstead, an iron washstand, four cane chairs, a clothes-rack, a coal-scuttle, a fender and irons and a square table on which lay a double desk. A bookcase had been made in an alcove by means of shelves of white wood. The bed was clothed with white bedclothes and a black and scarlet rug covered the foot. A little hand-mirror hung above the washstand and during the day a white-shaded lamp stood as the sole ornament of the mantelpiece. (*D* 107)

By the end, with Mrs. Sinico a suicide and Duffy fully cognizant of his part in her death, he can look forward—no matter how much the the world outside may beckon—to spending the rest of his life in this geometric cell to which he has condemned himself.

In *Chamber Music*, as in "A Painful Case," the wood is a place primarily of physical fulfillment, though those who see it as such—Mr. Duffy and the young man of the *Chamber Music* sequence—do so by projection rather than by person involvement. Mr. Duffy sees, and envies, the human figures lying "in the shadow of the wall of the Park," near the wood, if not in it; the young speaker of the *Chamber Music* sequence seeks to lure the young woman he is courting into the wood as in poem XX:

> In the dark pine-wood
> I would we lay,
> In deep cool shadow
> At noon of day.
>
> How sweet to lie there,
> Sweet to kiss,
> Where the great pine-forest
> Enaisled is!

In poem XXIV the girl's chamber is the scene of a pointless self-inspection (the narcissism noted previously) and the wood, by contrast, the scene of at least potential fulfillment:

> Silently she's combing,
> Combing her long hair,
> Silently and graciously,
> With many a pretty air.
>
> The sun is in the willow leaves
> And on the dappled grass,
> And still she's combing her long hair
> Before the looking-glass.

The implicaiton of the "still" of the second stanza is that the girl should not be detained by her own image, but should pay heed to the world outside the window and the young man who waits for her there. The chamber of this sequence of poems is typically the scene of self-delusion—and not only for the girl. In poem VI, the young man moves mistakenly back toward the maternal bosom (and perhaps also, like Stephen in chapter III of *A Portrait*, back toward the Church with its austerities), a bosom imaged in the the poem as a chamber:

> I would be ever in that heart
> (O soft I knock and soft entreat her!)
> Where only peace might be my part.
> Austerities were all the sweeter
> So I were ever in that heart.[86]

If the implication of the visits to the wood in *Chamber Music* is primarily sexual, the implication of Stephen's moment of religious ecstasy in the wood described in the final section of *A Portrait* is quite the opposite:

> ... he remembered an evening when he had dismounted from a borrowed creaking bicycle to pray to God in a wood near Malahide. He had lifted up his arms and spoken in ecstasy to the sombre nave of the trees, knowing that he stood on holy gound and in a holy hour. And when two constabularymen had come into sight round a bend in the gloomy road he had broken off his prayer to whistle loudly an air from the last pantomime. (*P* 232)

This recurring passage occurs in the very first version of *A Portrait*, the short story or sketch of 1904, in a much abbreviated form. In this version the interruption is not caused by constabularymen, and the context of the scene is different: "He ran through his measure like a spendthrift saint, astonishing many by ejaculatory fervours, offending many by airs of the cloister. One day in a wood near Malahide a labourer had marvelled to see a boy of fifteen praying in an ecstasy of Oriental posture."[87] In this scene—which occurs in all versions of *A Portrait*—the wood suggests the nature of Baudelaire's "Correspondences," in which both the mind and the senses come alive. The trees of the scene in *A Portrait*, in forming a "sombre nave" truly become "living columns" ("vivants piliers") in the " forests of symbols" (" forêts de symboles") of the book. For the painters of the 1890s, for many of whom the poem of Baudelaire's was a primary source, the forest or wood meant much the same thing as it does to Stephen, Gabriel, Duffy, and the young man of the *Chamber Music* sequence—a scene of renewal in several senses of the word— though the chamber perhaps meant something else.

In *The Wood* (ca. 1892) (Figure 25), a small canvas by Vuillard, three trees occur at nearly a right angle to the fourth and therefore suggest, with typical Symbolist obliqueness, that we are in the temple of nature. In the Nabi Paul Sérusier's *Incantation* (1890) (Figure 26) we are unmistakably there, for in this painting—with a literalness that contrasts sharply with that of *The Wood* (and which illustrates well the range of aesthetic solutions thought viable by Symbolist artists)—one figure kneels in supplication at the altar of nature while two others stand behind her, one with her hands folded. The bowls, and the flame spurting forth from the rock, suggest the symbolism of the mass. In spite of certain touches, which work against its prevailing verticality, such as the tilt of the head of one of the standing figures and the angle of certain trees, the impression of the painting is immediately hieratic; we know these figures stand, in Joyce's phrase, "on holy ground and in a holy hour." The woman in Munch's *The Voice* (1893) (Figure 27) stands rather than kneels, but the hour may be closer to that of Stephen's prayer, and the moment is certainly equally solemn. In the background, on the water, the light of the moon forms the cross which recurs so frequently in Munch's work. The trees are rigidly vertical. So, too, are the trees in Maurice Denis's *Le Soir Trinitaire* (Trinitarian Evening) (1891),[88] though the figures neither stand nor perform a ceremony: two of the three women are nude and seated on the grass, while the third, fully clothed in a dark dress, stands nearby. This work attains its suggestiveness subtly, through the title and the curving stream in the background, which suggests the Symbolist Way to unity and serves as a substitute in the symbolic scheme of the painting for the grove of trees in the Sérusier and the reflected moon in the Munch. The dress, as in the Munch, is contemporary. In another Denis, *The Muses* (1893), the grove of trees, solemn and hieratic, does appear, with the same diagonal as in Vuillard's *The Wood*. The muses sit in a park not unlike the Tuileries, and they also wear modern clothing.[89] The title of the work, as well as its setting, makes plain its relationship to the theme of the religion of art popular in the 1890s; in the recurring scene in Joyce, this same relationship is established by the details of the scene described, and by the context (in Stephen's development) in which it appears.

In these works the forest comes alive through the ceremonial presence of human beings; in other works of the period, the wood has a life of its own—an animistic one, frequently tinged strongly by sensuality. This sensual quality derives in part from Romantic work that influenced the Symbolists, such as Moritz von Schwind's *The Organic Life of Nature (Das Organische Leben der Natur)* (Figure 28), perhaps merely as a result, in the case of this illustration, of the attitude of the center figures. In Giovanni Segantini's proto-Surrealist *Evil Mothers* (also known as *Infanticide*) (1894) (Figure 29), the highly charged form of the woman seems to grow out of the tree, yet it is obviously human in a way the forms in *Das Organische Leben* are not. The hair of the girl of Art Nouveau has a similar relationship to the branches and leaves with which it is intertwined. An early etching of Klee's, *Maiden in Tree* (1930)[90] also depicts a young woman reclining on, yet somehow part of, a bare-branched tree. In Albert Weisgerber's somewhat later *Reclining Figure in a Mountainous Landscape* (1914) (Figure 30), the nude figure of the woman is separate from its surroundings but vastly out of proportion to them; the effect is to make of the woman a form equal to the landscape in which it lies, and thus comparable to the large nude in Klinger's *The Philosopher*.

In *A Portrait*, Stephen has two dreams that might be termed animistic, the second much friendlier than the first. Both show certain links with animistic landscape of the period. In chapter III—as a result of the intense guilt he feels from his sexual desires—he dreams of creatures in a field:

> Creatures were in the field; one, three, six: creatures were moving in the field, hither and thither. Goatish creatures with human faces, hornybrowed, lightly bearded and grey as india-rubber. The malice of evil glittered in their hard eyes, as they moved hither and thither, trailing their long tails behind them. A rictus of cruel malignity lit up greyly their old bony faces.... Soft language issued from their spittleless lips as they swished in slow circles round and round the field, winding hither and thither through the weeds, dragging their long tails amid the rattling canisters. They moved in slow circles, circling closer and closer to enclose, to enclose, soft language issuing from their lips, their long swishing tails besmeared with stale shite, thrusting upwards their terrific faces.... (*P* 137-138)

This unpleasant landscape of the mind is close in spirit to the neurotic world of Segantini or the early Klee work, but much closer in spatial conception to the intricate and also somewhat neurotic landscapes of the proto-Symbolist Rodolphe Bresdin, as, for instance, in the 1854 etching *The Comedy of*

Death,[91] for which Joyce's description of the tangled field and its inhabitants would do admirably: "A field of stiff weeds and thistles and tufted nettlebunches. Thick among the tufts of rank stiff growth lay battered canisters and clots and coils of solid excrement. A faint marshlight struggled upwards from all the ordure through the bristling greygreen weeds. An evil smell, faint and foul as the light, curled upwards sluggishly out of the canisters and from the stale crusted dung" (*P* 137).

A later vision, in chapter IV of *A Portrait*—just before the encounter with the girl on the beach—suggests a quieter, less sinister world, but one which is no less animistic. In this passage, Stephen hears a new path opening to him:

> It seemed to him that he heard notes of fitful music leaping upwards a tone and downwards a diminished fourth, upwards a tone and downwards a major third, like triple-branching flames leaping fitfully, flame after flame, out of a midnight wood. It was an elfin prelude, endless and formless; and, as it grew wilder and faster, the flames leaping out of time, he seemed to hear from under the boughs and grasses wild creatures racing, their feet pattering like rain upon the leaves. Their feet passed in pattering tumult over his mind, the feet of hares and rabbits, the feet of harts and hinds and antelopes, until he heard them no more.... (*P* 165)[92]

The romantic mood of the second vision makes of the forest an idyllic setting, a pastoral world, though somewhat speeded up by Stephen's anticipation. The forest of *Chamber Music,* as we have noted, is also a pastoral setting (in the wood and chamber of that sequence of poems we have a restatement of the traditional contrast of forest and court in the pastoral). This pastoral, romantic theme receives Symbolist treatment in a Munch woodcut of 1897, one of the earlier treatments of the subject in his *oeuvre,* entitled *To the Woods.*[93] We see a man and a nude woman from behind—arms about one another—as they walk away from us toward the wood, their figures seeming to blend with the landscape, as human figures can be made to disappear in films.

For Stephen to fulfill himself as artist and man, he must journey eastward; for Gabriel Conroy, as man if not as artist, the journey is in the opposite direction. What precedes it—the snow general over Ireland—is also general in Symbolist landscapes, though Symbolist artists typically describe it not as a landscape on which snow is falling but as one on which the snow has lain for some time. What sets such snow scenes aside from more naturalistic treatments of this subject is their suggestion that the frozen world of the painting will not long stay frozen—that the life beneath the snow will soon reassert itself.

This quality in Symbolist snow scenes sometimes is asserted in literary fashion by way of the title—as, for example, in Otto Geigenberger's *The Sleeping Tree,*[94] but more often than not it is a thing felt rather than told. A well-detailed winter landscape by the Finnish Symbolist Akseli Gallén-Kallela (1902)[95] with its snow-laden branches seen close up in the manner of the

Japanese artists, has this quality, and so does a winter landscape of the same year by the Swiss artist Cuno Amiet, though in the latter the treatment is more abstract.[96] In a winter scene by Munch from 1899 (Figure 31), in keeping with this theme, the mounds of snow seem about to come to life, to become organic or even human forms.

The tension in the Symbolist snow scene derives from the feeling that behind the smooth white surface of the snow something is beginning to move, to stir, to come to life; the tension between the smoothness of the surface and the feeling that that surface will break up, dissolve, or in some way reform itself accounts for the aesthetic interest of the painting. As primary forms resolve themselves into secondary, Wilde's remark that art is both surface and symbol finds new application. Immanence gives way to imminence, permanence to change.

Gabriel, at the end of "The Dead," also feels this suggestion in the scene from nature framed in the window of the hotel room he is sharing with his wife. We need not quote the long passage with which the story ends, but merely remark the fact that it is "against the lamplight" that Gabriel sees the flakes begin to fall—the lamplight which in "Araby," third story in the book and the last of the childhood group, strives vainly to unite earth and air. This passage from "The Dead"—and the story of which it is part—take their place with the great celebrations in the visual arts of the period, not only of the cycle of the seasons, but also of the cycle of life, one of the most striking of which (in sculpture at least) is a work by the sculptor of the Nabi group, Georges Lacombe: a bed of four sculptured panels which he did in wood in the early 1890s.

The subject of the panel at the foot of the bed is the birth of a child. The mother, lying partly on her long hair, lies to the right, her hand raised to her face, as a bearded man—a priest of some sort—delivers the baby. To the left, in garb like that of a nun, a woman stands praying. The panels on either side of the bed depict the beginning and the end of the cycle of life. In the one on the right a young couple makes love, and in the one on the left an old woman draws the shroud over the corpse of an old man. The head panel is an abstract rendering of the whole cycle in a traditional symbol—a serpent coiled about itself, its tail in its mouth, two loops forming, on the right, the eyes of a masklike face. Just as we must move about the bed to see the fulfillment of the cycle, beginning on the right and ending on the left, so we must move our eyes from right to left, counterclockwise, to read the meaning of the coiled serpent. But to infer that there is an end to the composition or its theme is of course not accurate—the end is the beginning, the beginning is the end.[97] And so it is with Gabriel lying in bed at the end of "The Dead," his journey westward a journey to rebirth; and so it is later, at the end of *Ulysses*, with the Blooms, lying at opposite ends of their bed, their positions suggesting the cycle of death and rebirth—that serpent of tradition—affirming the affirmatives with which the work ends: "yes I said yes I will yes."

For Gabriel, rejuvenation is imagined in terms of the exterior world. The interior world—the hotel room—suggests more hope than life. Time and again, the interior setting in Joyce's work suggests the opposite of what it means in the work of so many artists of the 1890s. To understand how Joyce's work compares with Symbolist art and literature, it is necessary also to understand how it differs. To the Nabi artists, for instance, the interior had the same importance as the still life to the Cubists, or the scene of city life to the Impressionists; in the interior lay one of the means for them to realize the aims of their aesthetic program. The thematic basis of this program is summed up in part by a passage from an essay by Maurice Maeterlinck:

> I have come to believe that an old man seated in his armchair, simply waiting beneath the lamp, listening without knowing it to all the eternal laws which govern his household, interpreting without understanding it what there is in doors and windows and in the small voice of the light, submitting to the presence of his soul and his destiny, inclining slightly his head, without suspecting all the forces of this world intervening and watching over [him] in the room like attentive servants... —I have come to believe that this motionless old man lives in reality a life more profound, more human and more universal than the lover who strangles his mistress, the captain who wins a victory or "the husband who avenges his honor."[98]

The Nabis managed sometimes to suggest these eternal laws at work in interiors without people. No one appears in *Mystery*, the little canvas by Vuillard (ca. 1895) (Figure 2), or in *The Two Doors*, an earlier interior by the same artist (1891), in which the spectator is invited to inspect what appears to be an empty room. In the way it captures the imagination with its simple conception, the latter scene particularly suggests the compelling nature of eternal laws to which, as Maeterlinck indicates, man must submit himself.[99]

In Maeterlinck's image of the forces of the eternal at work, an old man sits beneath a lamp; in Nabi interiors, a figure also usually appears, often engaged in a simple activity which indicates that he or she is attuned to the compelling rhythm of the universe. In another small canvas by Vuillard (ca. 1892),[100] a woman sits with her back to the spectator, sewing quietly. Absorbed in her task, she is also, as a figure, absorbed by the space of which she is part; her loss of individuality and discreteness is appropriate in that it reflects her submission to the forces operating upon her. Another Vuillard interior (ca. 1890-1892)[101] shows two women standing at a linen closet; by their attitude they seem to be engaged in some sort of religious ritual, an impression reinforced by the cross suggested on the wall in the left half of the canvas. As in Sérusier's *Incantation* (Figure 26), the mood is solemn, hieratic, though it is achieved by subtler, more painterly means. In Denis's *Our Spirits, with Slow Gestures (Nos Âmes, en des gestes lents)* (1911),[102] the activity is musical: a woman stands pensively at the piano, holding a rose; beneath a small lamp—that artificial light which Maeterlinck mentions and which occurs in so much Nabi work—a man sits playing; a few flowers in the upper right complete the composition. The interest of the work is decorative—the details of the brocade and the lamp give a sure indication of that—but also, as the title indicates, more than that. In *Les Revenants de Musique,* an early Beardsley drawing, visionary figures inspired by music appear before a seated, slouching, weary-looking young man.[103] Music as a means to communicate the otherwise incommunicable, music as the supreme art or, at any rate, as the art which more than any other could meaningfully inform literature, is so endemic to the period as to require no special comment.

In Joyce's work—if we exclude the description of Duffy's room—there is no parallel to the interior without figures, but there are a sufficient number of scenes involving figures, frequently engaged in musical activity, which stand apart because of their spatial qualities, to invite comparison with the Symbolist interior with figures. One such scene occurs in *Stephen Hero,* when Stephen, weary as Beardsley's young man, sits in a room with a typically gloomy *fin-de-siècle* air:

> He was hardly unhappy and yet not happy. His moods were still waited upon and courted and set down in phrases of prose and verse: and when the soles of his feet were too tired or his mood too dim a memory or too timid a hope, he would wander into the long lofty dusty drawing-room and sit at the piano while the sunless dusk enwrapped him. . . . The chords that floated towards the cobwebs and rubbish and floated vainly to the dust-strewn windows were the meaningless voices of his perturbation and all they could do was flow in meaningless succession through all the chambers of sentience. He breathed an air of tombs. (*S* 162)

In Joyce the making of music does not always serve the same function as in the work by Denis or in much other Symbolist work; instead of serving to suggest the invisible links between man and the universe, it frequently suggests the isolation of the individual from such links. In this passage the interior setting suggests the oppressive atmosphere of the tomb; the music, by floating outwards, suggests the possibility of escape from this oppressive atmosphere—the possibility of establishing meaningful connection with the universe—but Stephen seems to miss the cue it provides.

The second poem of *Chamber Music* provides an instance of a character, also in an interior setting, missing a similar cue, when the girl of the sequence sits idly at the piano and does not go outdoors where love is:

> The old piano plays an air,
>   Sedate and slow and gay;
> She bends upon the yellow keys,
>   Her head inclines this way.
>
> Shy thoughts and grave wide eyes and hands
>   That wander as they list—
> The twilight turns to darker blue
>   With lights of amethyst.

In *Dubliners,* in "Clay," in a scene of painful irony (though without a strong spatial quality), Maria sings a song, the vast inappropriateness of which is perhaps apparent even to her, and in "The Dead," in a scene of multiple ironies (and with the strong spatial quality that characterizes the whole story), Gabriel hears in Aunt Julia's song both what is there and what he would like to hear: "Her voice, strong and clear in tone, attacked with great spirit the runs which embellish the air and though she sang very rapidly she did not miss even the smallest of the grace notes. To follow the voice, without looking at the singer's face, was to feel and share the excitement of swift and secure flight"(*D* 193). At the end of "The Boarding House" there is no music, but there is, in that description of Polly in the bedroom, waiting for the word from downstairs, the same sense of oppressiveness, of life wasted or misunderstood, that pervades other such interior scenes in Joyce: "She waited on patiently, almost cheerfully, without alarm, her memories gradually giving place to hopes and visions of the future. Her hopes and visions were so intricate that she no longer saw the white pillows on which her gaze was fixed or remembered that she was waiting for anything" (*D* 68).

In Maeterlinck's description of an old man in a room, feeling the operation of invisible forces upon himself, there is none of the oppressiveness which characterizes such scenes in early Joyce. To Maeterlinck, and to certain of the Nabis who gained inspiration and support from his work, the interior setting was the one in which the imagination functioned best: it was the ideal setting for inner revelation. For Joyce, it served chiefly to suggest the limits sometimes placed upon the imagination, and the ideal setting for an imaginative revelation is much more the outdoors than the in. When, in *A Portrait,* Stephen, lying in his bed, turns away from the ordinary life outside his window, he, after all, produces only the villanelle.

This distinction between experiences outside and in is not to be observed, however, by the time we reach *Ulysses.* There, the important moments inside— in newspaper office, lying-in hospital, whorehouse, or Bloom's house—are balanced by the important moments outside—on street or strand, in graveyard or field—but by then, we have also entered into a wholly different aesthetic world. In "The Sirens" episode, music is not thematic embellishment or adumbration but the very essence of the chapter, both in language and in narrative technique. In that episode, as in others throughout the volume, subject, theme, and technique are inextricably interwoven by Joyce in a manner much more complex than that of the earlier work. In *Ulysses* as a whole the significant correspondences to the plastic arts are thus not those of imagery, but of technique.

In Maeterlinck's description of an old man in a room, feeling the operation of invisible forces upon himself, there is none of the oppressiveness which characterizes such scenes in early Joyce. To Maeterlinck, and to certain of the Nabis who gained inspiration and support from his work, the interior setting was the one in which the imagination functioned best: it was the ideal setting for inner revelation. For Joyce, it served chiefly to suggest the limits sometimes placed upon the imagination, and the ideal setting for an imaginative revelation is much more the outdoors than the in. When, in *A Portrait,* Stephen, lying in his bed, turns away from the ordinary life outside his window, he, after all, produces only the villanelle.

This distinction between experiences outside and in is not to be observed, however, by the time we reach *Ulysses*. There, the important moments inside— in newspaper office, lying-in hospital, whorehouse, or Bloom's house—are balanced by the important moments outside—on street or strand, in graveyard or field—but by then, we have also entered into a wholly different aesthetic world. In "The Sirens" episode, music is not thematic embellishment or adumbration but the very essence of the chapter, both in language and in narrative technique. In that episode, as in others throughout the volume, subject, theme, and technique are inextricably woven by Joyce in a manner much more complex than that of the earlier work. In *Ulysses* as a whole the significant correspondences to the plastic arts are thus not those of imagery, but of technique.

3

Ulysses, Cubism, and Other Movements in Modern Art

The year 1907 marks an important point in the development of modern art, for it was in the spring of that year that Picasso completed the masterpiece which as surely as any other single work introduces the twentieth century: *Les Demoiselles d'Avignon* (Figure 32). In the words of Robert Rosenblum, it "mirrors the past and proclaims the future, for it both resumes an earlier tradition and begins a new one."[1] This great work, like *Ulysses,* sums up all that precedes it and then takes the art it represents into a new phase; like the movement it heralds—and again like *Ulysses*—it presents an historical view of the representation of reality in Western art and also provides a criticism of it; finally, like *Ulysses,* it requires of those who wish to experience it a willingness to look at things anew, to see them fresh, to participate, as it were, in the very process by which they are created.

Before we explore in detail the various levels of the relationship between Joyce's work and Cubism, it might be well to review just what Cubism represented in the development of modern art—what its contribution was, and where that contribution fitted in. From 1906, when Cézanne died and Picasso began the first studies for what was to become *Les Demoiselles,* to 1914, when war broke out and the Cubist group broke up, the premises of Cubism gradually became part of the common vocabulary of art. Its most fundamental assertion was that the artist's imagination is a more valid criterion for the measurement of artistic achievement than any other standard, in particular the proximity of what he has created to some external or objective standard of reality. The assertion of this standard—which was to become the strongest common element among the various segments of the modern movement in the visual arts—involved, among other things, the rejection of practically every major principle established in the Renaissance and perpetuated by all important artists from then until at least the middle of the nineteenth century. Fixed spatial or temporal relationships—all the various devices which together formed the basis of pictorial illusionism—were called into question, to create, again in Robert Rosenblum's words, "an artistic language of intentional ambiguity."[2] The innovations of the Cubists extended even to the very materials of the work of art, which, through collage (devised by 1912), came ultimately to include practically anything. Indeed, in only one major respect did the Cubists remain anchored in tradition—in their not giving up the subject as did Kandinsky and others who worked in an even more nonobjective manner; yet this distinction is less significant than at first it may seem when one confronts works from the phase of analytical Cubism, for here the subject is all but lost in the complex grid of intersecting planes that makes up the picture surface.

The subject matter of Cubism consists primarily of scenes or emblems of the *vie de Bohème* as it was lived in the first decade of the century by the group surrounding Picasso and Braque in Paris: portraits of the artist or his friends, themselves artists or poets or dealers; scenes of studio or café life—the two poles of existence for the young artists—less depicted than suggested by selected details; and still life of infinite formal variety, often made up of details of studio or café, but including also, especially after the development of collage, scraps of paper of various kinds, and words, sometimes used as objects and sometimes used specifically for the meanings they convey. This is a subject matter related both to the world of the artist and to the world of Paris in which the artists lived: more than any previous movement in art, including Impressionism, Cubism has an urban subject matter.[3] Like *Ulysses,* it fuses in a complex and ironic way nineteenth-century aestheticism—the notion of art for art's sake—with a fragmented subject matter derived from twentieth century urban existence. Like *Ulysses,* it makes of these materials something at once realistic—in the commonly accepted sense of that which is within the range of perceivable reality—and formally daring—in fact radical in its departure from artistic conventions.

It is ironical, considering the overwhelming importance of Cubism to the development of twentieth-century art—indeed, to the twentieth-century way of *seeing*—that no literary movement *per se* accompanied its development. Certain poets may fairly be called Cubist, at least in some of their work (Apollinaire is a major example)[4] but there is no literary movement which may be called Cubist in the sense that there are literary movements connected with Futurism, with Dadaism, and especially with Surrealism. All of these movements share with Cubism certain techniques and principles—indeed were influenced by Cubism in many fundamental respects—yet they have their literary counterparts and Cubism by and large does not.

Be this as it may, it is possible to identify in many major literary works of the modern period qualities which are both important to these works and important to Cubism. The Cantos of Pound, Eliot's *The Waste Land,* the poetry of William Carlos Williams and e.e. cummings—the list is long. *Ulysses,* conceived and executed at the very moment in the history of art when the revolution which was Cubism was being felt most generally, also provides a good case in point, for in at least three major respects *Ulysses* reflects the aesthetic principles of Cubism: (1) it takes an approach to narrative comparable to the temporal-spatial conceptions of Cubism; (2) it uses materials and techniques approximating those of collage; and (3) it comprises within itself a criticism of all previous art, thereby raising fundamental questions about the nature of art and about the creative process.

It is by now a widely accepted view that *Ulysses* is in fact two novels. One is the realistic novel *par excellence*—the culminating statement of nineteenth century psychological realism, incorporating not only detailed renderings of conversation, but also exact though highly subjective depictions of the surroundings and the thoughts of the major characters. The other novel is the one which goes beyond realism to include various authorial ironies which both complicate and in some respects tend to destroy the basic line of the narrative, which is—the intentional obscurities of "stream-of-consciousness" notwithstanding—relatively straightforward up to the point these ironies begin. The first *Ulysses* corresponds roughly to the first quarter of the novel, the second, more "experimental" *Ulysses,* to the remainder. The nature of this difference, and of the process by which it was created, has been dealt with elsewhere.[5] Its importance to this study is that many of the most pointed analogies between *Ulysses,* Cubism, and other movements in modern art occur in the more experimental, less "realistic," portion of the text.

The imagery of the earlier works, on the other hand, remains pervasive throughout. Joyce not only wrote in splendid detail about the Dublin of June 1904, he also continued to see Dublin and its people as he had learned to see them then. Thus, in "Proteus," as Stephen strolls on the strand, the weeds he sees take on the qualities of the girl with long flowing hair he sees at the end of chapter IV of *A Portrait:*

> Under the upswelling tide he saw the writhing weeds lift languidly and sway reluctant arms, hising up their petticoats, in whispering water swaying and upturning coy silver fronds. Day by day: night by night: Lifted, flooded and let fall. Lord, they are weary: and, whispered to, they sigh. Saint Ambrose heard it, sigh of leaves and waves, waiting, awaiting the fullness of their times.... (*U* 49.35)

In this passage, in keeping with the theme of metamorphosis so important to this episode, it is the weeds which take on the qualities of the girl rather than, as in *A Portrait,* the girl who takes on the qualities of the animal or vegetable world, but the imagery is still visually the same—the sensuous, undulating, seemingly never-ending repetition of forms so characteristic of Art Nouveau.

Again, in "Scylla and Charybdis," the view of the artist as necromancer— as priest of the imagination—so notable in *A Portrait* and elsewhere in early Joyce occurs to Stephen while among his elders:

Yogeybogeybox in Dawson chambers *Isis Unveiled.* Their Pali book we tried to pawn. Crosslegged under an umbrel umbershoot he thrones an Aztec logos, functioning on astral levels, their oversoul, mahamahatma. The faithful hermetists await the light, ripe for chelaship, ringroundabout him. Louis H. Victory. T. Caulfield Irwin. Lotus ladies tend them i'the eyes, their pineal glands aglow. Filled with his god he thrones, Buddh under plantain. Gulfer of souls, engulfer. Hesouls, shesouls, shoals of souls. Engulfed with wailing creecries, whirled, whirling, they bewail. (*U* 191.37-192.5)

In this passage this view is subjected to considerable mockery—Stephen's Paris experiences having altered his opinion of artistic priesthood somewhat—yet the view of the artist it contains is essentially the same as that we have seen before.

Other passages of *Ulysses* provide similar instances of its continuity with the imagery of the earlier works (for instance, those which carry on the analogy between Stephen and Christ begun in *A Portrait,* supporting yet another view of the artist in this period),[6] but despite this continuity it is less in the area of imagery and more in the area of techniques of rendering reality that significant analogies between Joyce's work and modern art occur after 1914. Of particular interest in this regard are the temporal and spatial ambiguities provided by Cubism.

The fixed moment in time of Impressionist painting (we think of Monet in his haystack series, or in his series on the Rouen Cathedral, moving from canvas to canvas at different times of day, to capture as precisely as possible the light of that particular moment) gives way by the time of the Cubists to a deliberate impreciseness—not so much the universal time of allegorical or classical landscape as ambiguous time. If the aim of the Impressionists was to capture the moment as precisely as they could, rendering light in the atmosphere at particular times of day, the aim of the Cubists—in this respect influenced by the post-Impressionists and Cézanne—lay elsewhere, particular time being largely diffused in their work by the constantly shifting priorities of a more complex treatment of space. "It is the social function of great poets and artists," Apollinaire noted in "The Cubist Painters," "to renew continually the appearance nature has for the eyes of men."[7] In this renewal on the part of the Cubists time is ambiguous but still important, especially for its fusion of past and present in one composite whole.

The fusion shows itself early, in the seminal *Les Demoiselles d'Avignon,* where Picasso brings together in one canvas figures drawn from disparate traditions and different times—Egyptian (with a touch of hieratic Greek and also of the Tahitian Gauguin) to the left side of the composition, African primitive in the two figures stacked to the right, and, in tribute to his Spanish roots, Iberian primitive in the middle pair. History and prehistory come together here on equal ground, and, if the artist, in keeping with the same antihistorical feelings which animated so many artists of the early modern period, seems inclined more toward the primitive than the refined, he is at least acknowledging his artistic debts as well as his departures. The figure on the left is a reference point to an artistic tradition which the rest of the painting eschews, but our understanding of this eschewal depends upon the apposition of this figure (which seems, in profile, to be looking at the others) to the more primitive pairs.[3]

If *Les Demoiselles d'Avignon* illustrates in seminal form the fusion of past and present in Cubist art, it is with the development of collage, some five years later, that this element of temporal apposition begins to occur more universally. Work from the period between *Les Demoiselles*—which is to say, the earliest phase of Cubism—and the spring of 1912, when collage first occurred, sustains the notion of temporal ambiguity contained in Picasso's seminal work, but generally not the notion of temporal apposition. Cubist work of the so-called analytical phase, which reached its peak just prior to the creation of collage, is concerned primarily with the destruction of the object and its reassemblage as a series of planes on the picture surface. Collage, however, took significantly further these spatial explorations by introducing into the composition of the work of art new materials which shortly yielded temporal as well as spatial complexities of a new order. The new materials—pieces of oil cloth or grains of sand, or printed matter in the form of portions of sheet music and newspapers—grew logically out of the purely painted work of the analytical phase, and in fact served more thoroughly than any of that work to anchor the Cubist achievement in the world of reality, to which it is always related. The lines and shapes and textures of Cubist collage, though abstract in feeling, refer to a world of objects which the spectator can recognize outside the boundaries of the work of art. In this reference system it is the newspaper fragments which frequently (and fittingly enough) provide the temporal information and which serve to suggest the fusion of past and present in the work of art.

In the most general sense all the newspaper fragments in Cubist collage provide temporal information, if only by suggesting the fleeting nature of time in comparison with the work of art. Thus the frequent use—by Picasso for example—of mastheads from *Le Journal* which stress the first four letters of the name.[9] More specifically, in such work as *The Cups* by Juan Gris (1914),[10] the newspaper photographs make a more complicated commentary on permanence and impermanence, showing, as they do, a statue on the Place de la Concorde before it is stripped of its electoral notices and after. Because such displays of posted notices were part of the inspiration for collage *(papiers collés)*, these photographs and the fragment of an article they illustrate provide ironic comment on the method of collage, which is the very reverse of the stripping process which has occurred. Past and present are fused in a conventional way in the work, to make an ironic comment on what was then an unconventional form of art. Similar examples may be found both in Dadaist and in Surrealist work.[11]

In *Ulysses* specific time is quite obviously of much more importance than it ever is in Cubist or Cubist-influenced collage, the novel depending for one measure of its consonance upon the complicated and very precise time scheme of the various episodes. This scheme is both sequential (one episode following another in time as we follow each major character) and simultaneous (the time sequence duplicated to show us the correspondence among events in the lives of the major—and, in "Wandering Rocks," some minor—characters). Joyce, like the Impressionists, is concerned with specific moments in time throughout the day, though for him the intervals between moments—when events are not recorded, but implied—are as important in some respects as the moments themselves. Within this temporal scheme, however, occurs also a continual juxtaposition of past (in the form of the subconscious or unconscious thoughts of the characters) and present (in the form of their conscious thoughts or utterances). Although these thoughts and utterances occur sequentially in the text, they have the same quality of simultaneity to be found in the various fragments which make up Cubist and Cubist-influenced collage. That is, though we may read them in sequence, we must take them as occurring simultaneously. Thus, for example, Bloom surveys the tombstones at Paddy Dignam's funeral and, in the midst of several platitudinous and humorous thoughts, remembers Molly "wanting to do it at the window" (*U* 108.19), and Stephen in the library scene, later in the day, in what constitutes three virtually simultaneous thoughts rendered consecutively, thinks of himself at Clongowes ("a child Conmee saved from pandies"—*U* 190.1), of his various selves ("I, I and I.I."—*U* 190.2), and of his debt to A.E. ("A.E., I.O.U.—*U* 190.3). The juxtaposition of such elements in the text has typically the same ironic effect as in collage, one element impinging upon another and influencing our interpretation of the whole.

In the earlier, more realistic portion of *Ulysses* from which my examples have been drawn—beginning with "Telemachus" and going through "Hades" (but including also "Lestrygonians" and much of "Scylla and Charybdis")—the juxtaposition within the framework of a developing "stream-of-consciousness" technique, which depends heavily upon such ironic effects for its success. In the remainder of the text—the more "experimental" portion, beginning somewhat tentatively in "Aeolus" and "Scylla" and moving out full stride in "Sirens" and "Cyclops"—the technique of juxtaposition is complicated by the intrusion of various authorial ironies in the voice or persona of the "arranger," David Hayman's good term.[12] These authorial ironies constitute, in different styles, additions to the main text or replications of it, and they frequently refer to different times than that main text. This juxtaposition of diverse temporal elements is if anything even more ironic in effect than that in the opening episodes of the novel. Furthermore, it is as much spatial in form—in the sense that Joseph Frank intended that term in his seminal essay "Spatial Form in Modern Literature"—as temporal.[13]

"Cyclops" provides the best example of the latter. In this episode, in which the main narrative is in the first person, in the style of the anonymous friend of the Citizen who has an argument with Bloom, the various interpolated passages (33 in all) not only contrast in style and substance with the main narrative but also differ, sometimes pointedly, in time. Thus in the second such passage, beginning "In Inisfail the fair there lies a land" (*U* 293.38), we are in a medieval or quasimedieval setting—of "murmuring waters, fishful streams"— in marked contrast with the tawdry barroom of the main narrative. The medieval world suggested here may be the spiritual antecedent to the shopworn heroism of the Citizen, but the passage does not so much further the scene it comments on as interrupt it. Its relationship to the main narrative depends upon the set of contrasts it suggests, which include, perhaps most obviously, that of time. However, because this passage is set beside that main narrative, not integrated with it, their relationship is fundamentally spatial, not temporal. Like the seemingly disjointed fragments of Cubist collage, it attains significance as much by dissimilarity as similarity to its surrounding elements. In the aggregate, these bardlike interpolations in "Cyclops" do achieve a sort of continuity (if we read them in sequence, omitting the main text), but it is still chiefly a continuity of style or tone, not of events, and this continuity is ultimately broken by the introduction of other, more contemporary, styles.

"Oxen of the Sun" is superficially similar in technique, in that the episode consists of a series of styles which carry the narrative a few steps forward at the same time that they suggest the history of English prose; but, however complicated or variegated its time, it lacks the quality of spatiality of "Cyclops." Furthermore, its various styles are not interpolations, but themselves a sequential substitute for the main narrative—however, at this point in the book, that may be defined. "Nausikää" and "Wandering Rocks" on the other hand have a strong spatial quality. The first achieves this quality by the juxtaposition of diverse elements, especially at the very end of the episode, and the second achieves it by means of its succession of miniature scenes, each related, throughout Dublin. However, the juxtaposed elements in "Nausikää" all occur at the same time, and the scenes of "Rocks," except for the carry-over lines, are subtly progressive. In "Eumaeus," "Ithaca," and "Penelope" there is less a juxtaposition of diverse temporal elements than a fusion or blending of such elements into a composite whole (in "Ithaca" this blending is achieved by the device of the questions), perhaps in keeping with the fusion Bloom seeks in the *Nostos*. Of all the other episodes of the more experimental portion of *Ulysses*, "Aeolus" probably comes closest to the temporal-spatial juxtapositions of "Cyclops" and hence to the same sort of juxtaposition in collage. In "Aeolus," the effect is achieved not with interpolated passages but with the headlines or captions. These elements, like the various segments of "Oxen," are progressive in style and hence, by inference, in time, but they are also in distinct contrast, both in style and in tone, to the text in which they are interpolated. Again, as in the case of the "Cyclops" interpolations, they achieve significance and ironic effect as much by their dissimilarity to surrounding elements as by their similarity.

The temporal and spatial ambiguities of Cubism are created from extremely small units, fragments which, especially in collage, frequently constitute the throwaways of our civilization. In collage these small bits of reality constantly suggest larger things—a clef all of music, a few parallel lines the frets of a guitar, the word "BAL" the *bals publics* frequented by the painters and their friends. Words have thematic as well as spatial significance in these compositions: they serve in various ways to balance the compositions of which they are part, but they also add to them a significance which they would otherwise not have. They provide thematic as well as temporal diversity, and most often they come from that world of popular culture which in *Ulysses* is so important a part of the fabric of the novel.

It is possible in fact to identify the specific aspects of popular culture from which the verbal element of Cubist collage is derived. In the work of Picasso—in this respect Picasso's work is merely typical of the work of other members of the Cubist movement—Robert Rosenblum has identified as important not only newspaper mastheads, headlines, and captions, but also brand names, labels, advertisements, and posters, all of which, like the newspaper headlines of "Aeolus," play their parts in *Ulysses*. In direct reference to music, popular songs dominate (Picasso's "MA JOLIE," from a popular song of 1911, is perhaps the most famous example); such references, as in *Ulysses*, give us a sense of the *ambiance* of the painters' (or characters') lives, and also reflect directly the environment (urban, kaleidoscopic, typographical) from which their art is drawn.[14]

In *Ulysses* the whole rendering of reality known generally by the term stream-of-consciousness is based upon the fragment, or the syntactical element commonly given that name. Never before in the history of prose fiction had so much depended upon so little; these small bits of reality, taken together, make up a world. The nature of the fragments varies of course from Stephen to Bloom to Molly to other characters—according to differences of age, intelligence, experience, compassion, and Joyce's narrative strategy—but the substratum of the narrative is built of units which, were we to encounter them elsewhere, we would call incomplete. Furthermore, these units, which comprise one way or another the flow of each character's thoughts, resemble in substance as well as in form the verbal fragments which we see in Cubist collage. The fragments in Cubist collage do not suggest some deeper psychological reality nor do they form part of a continuous narrative, but in other respects they are quite similar in their aesthetic effects to the verbal fragments of Joyce. In particular, both sets of fragments succeed in suggesting, by what is often the most minimal means, values or qualities much larger than themselves. In this they share, in their respective art forms, an associative function important to their integrity as units in a work of art. The fragments in Cubist collage achieve this significance by their recurrence in a series of related compositions, just as the fragments of *Ulysses* achieve significance by their recurrence in the various episodes which comprise that work. In addition, because the open spaces of collage, like those in Cézanne's late works, have nearly as much significance to the compositions in which they occur as the filled ones, it is also true of collage and *Ulysses* that, in each, what is *not* represented or suggested is as important to our understanding of the work as what *is* represented or suggested. As in music, the rests are as important as the notes.[15]

As a matter of fact, the techniques of collage and of *Ulysses* may have a common root which would help to explain these similarities. The fragment in Cubist work derives in large measure, as the history of the development of modernism in the visual arts has come to be seen, from Impressionism by way of the post-Impressionists and Cézanne. The striated Impressionist stroke, developed in order to render more precisely the effects of light in the atmosphere, led to a vision of reality at odds with the essentially naturalistic vision of the painters who began working in this manner. The striated stroke, picked up by such painters as Seurat, Van Gogh and Gauguin, became, along with new theories of color, virtually an end in itself. In the hands of Cézanne, who used it to create his own shorthand version of reality, it most certainly did. Because Cézanne's late work was especially influential upon the Cubists' earliest efforts, we can trace a direct line from it to the early Cubist canvasses of Picasso and Braque; and thus, by extension, from the striated stroke of the Impressionists to the flat series of planes which are the formal mark of analytical Cubism and, in a sense as well, a primary source of the nonobjective manner in much of modern art. The scientific rendering of light by the Impressionists and Post-Impressionists thus ultimately becomes pure painting *(peinture-peinture)*—reality fully adjusted to the requirements of the artistic imagination.[16]

The stream-of-consciousness technique, as it developed in Joyce's work, also has roots in Impressionism—in the Impressionistic prose techniques common to *A Portrait of the Artist* and to work which was of influence on it. When we say that the first page of *Ulysses* grows out of the last pages of *A Portrait*—Stephen's fragmented diary entries leading to the fragmented thoughts of Stephen in the *Telemachia*—that is another way of saying that stream-of-consciousness begins in Impressionism. Impressionist prose is by its very nature disjointed in effect—a series of shimmering fragments which, taken as a whole, succeed in suggesting the flow of sensations or of thought. Various as their authors may be, such techniques in prose have as a common denominator a reliance upon fragmented imagery which is often reflected in fragmented syntax. In Impressionist prose as in Impressionist painting, the whole is quite obviously the sum of its parts, but the parts very frequently threaten the integrity of the whole—especially in Impressionist prose. If *A Portrait* is a great Impressionist novel, it is so specifically because Joyce never allows the overall integrity of the novel to be sacrificed to the parts, but even *A Portrait* has been seriously criticized for its lack of consonance.[17]

Because Impressionism is a common source of Joyce's stream-of-consciousness technique and of the technique of fragmentation devised by the Cubists, Joyce's expression of obligation for his technique to Édouard Dujardin (an expression of obligation that was once seen as diversionary or at least somewhat misleading) seems especially fitting. *Les Lauriers sont coupés,* published first in book form in 1888, after Impressionist painting had reached its zenith, is in many respects the Impresssionist novel *par excellence*—a series of vivid impressions of Paris in the 1880s which clearly reflects the Impressionist way of seeing things. Consider the very opening of the novel, which describes a Paris evening with the protagonist of the novel in its midst:

> Evening light of sunset, air far away, deep skies; a ferment of crowds, noises, shadows; spaces stretched out endlessly; a listless evening.
> And, from the chaos of appearance, in this time of all times, this place of places, amid the illusions of things self-begotten and self-conceived, one among others, one like the others yet distinct from them, the same and yet one more, from the infinity of possible lives, I arise.[18]

This passage, which Joyce particularly cited in discussing the "uninterrupted unrolling *(déroulement ininterrompu)*" of thought in Dujardin's novel,[19] is also a paradigm of the aesthetic experience offered by Impressionist prose and painting. It begins with a general sense of the light of the occasion and the sky in the background and then progresses to a more detailed perception of details and of mood. This passage also illustrates well a feature common to Dujardin's prose in *Les Lauriers sont coupés,* Joyce's prose in *A Portrait,* and much other prose that is labelled Impressionist: the process of perception is rendered not only by fragmenting the images, but also by repeating them in different syntactical forms. This is the equivalent in prose of the practice of Impressionist painters of placing dabs of color next to each other to suggest the shape of an object or person. The viewer must in effect reassemble the features of the object or person when he studies the canvas.

This process of perception is summed up by Dujardin's narrator when he says (immediately after the passage above) that "from the chaos of appearance" comes a specific time and place in which he finds himself: "So time and place come to a point; it is the Now and Here, this hour that is striking, and all around me life... "—a description which Joyce perhaps echoes in Stephen's line in "Aeolus," "Let there be life" (*U* 145.10). The details or parts come together to form an aesthetic whole which describes, in the tradition of naturalism, a specific time and place. Dujardin's novel, which is in some respects closely related to Joyce's work in its imagery, is also related to it in technique. To the extent that Impressionism is important to that technique, it may also be said to be important to Joyce's sense of time and place, rendered in Impressionist detail, in *Ulysses.*

If Impressionism provides a common source for the stream technique of *Ulysses* and for the technique of signs used by the Cubists, the headlines or captions which Joyce interpolated into the narrative of "Aeolus," after having done it once in straight narrative fashion, may represent a specific instance of Cubist influence upon Joyce's technique in the novel. These elements were entered not long before the novel was published and after Joyce had moved to Paris at the beginning of the Twenties. Michael Groden dates the interpolation of these elements into the narrative as occurring between August and October in 1921, when Joyce received the third page proofs.[20] Beginning in 1915, Joyce had spent the war years in Zurich and then, after a brief return to Trieste, had arrived in Paris by July 8, 1920, to remain for nearly the rest of his life. In either Zurich or Paris (or even possibly in Trieste, by the end of the Teens), Joyce might have been exposed to the Cubist technique of using headlines and captions in collage; by 1920 these techniques, first incorporated into Cubist work in 1912, had become part of the common vocabulary of the artistic avant-garde. The Futurists adopted the technique shortly after the Cubists first made use of it, but, perhaps more importantly to Joyce, the Dadaists also made use of it, along with other highly inventive typographical experiments, in Zurich during the time that Joyce lived there during the war.

In April 1916, the word *dada* was "discovered" and given to the new movement taking shape in Zurich which was at once an outgrowth of, and a reaction to, Cubism and Futurism.[21] February of that year saw the opening of Hugo Ball's Cabaret Voltaire, and March the first public reading of a simultaneous poem (by various hands) at the Cabaret. In June came the first and only publication of *Cabaret Voltaire,* with a preface by Ball, in which the word *dada* was used publicly for the first time. Contributors included Apollinaire, Arp, Cendrars, Richard Huelsenbeck, Kandinsky, Marinetti, Modigliani, Picasso, and Tristan Tzara. The first Dada soirée came on July 14, on which occasion Tzara read the first Dadaist manifesto and Hugo Ball read a *Lautgedichte,* or "sound-poem," of the sort already composed by the Futurists, but soon to be identified particularly with the Dada movement. From the very first, to a remarkable degree, the Dadaists were preoccupied with words— words in new contexts which robbed them of traditional meaning, words which were chosen randomly to represent new concepts, and words used (as the Cubists had often used them in their compositions) for spatial effect, which sometimes underscored what they signified and sometimes not. In keeping with these practices, the 1918 Dadaist manifesto, published by Huelsenbeck in Berlin, contained important subhead material, as well as many words capitalized in the text.[22] "DADA" itself receives such emphasis, followed shortly by "BRUITISTISCHE Gedicht," "SIMULTANISTISCHE Gedicht," and "STATISCHE Gedicht"—three types of poetry which the Dadaists encouraged, all developed by Tzara, Ball, and others in Zurich two years before. The first (derived from Futurism and invented by Ball) involved pure sounds represented phonetically; the second, a combination of randomly chosen lines and phonetic sounds, recited simultaneously; the third (especially attributable to Tzara), a series of randomly chosen phrases which could be rearranged to suit the needs of the occasion. In connection with collage and its techniques, it is significant for this last that Tzara recommended beginning with a newspaper:

> To make a dadaist poem
> Take a newspaper.
> Take a pair of scissors.
> Choose an article as long as you are planning to make
>   your poem.
> Cut out the article.
> Then cut out each of the words that make up this article
>   and put them in a bag.
> Shake it gently.
> Then take out the scraps one after the other in the
>   order in which they left the bag.
> Copy conscientiously.
> The poem will be like you.[23]

The randomness (also characteristic of Cubist and Futurist collage) is pure Dada; the satire of aestheticism, and the newpaper source, suggest strongly the technique of Joyce in "Aeolus."[24]

Joyce began by adding the headlines or captions to the left of the *placards* (galley proofs) which he received from the printer.[25] His initial list, while certainly far from random, has the literal quality of newspaper headlines or captions and an ironic effect much like that of the same elements in Cubist and Dadaist work: the reader must make the connection for himself. Revisions in this material in successive proofsheets as the weeks go on enliven "the original subheads...," as Groden puts it, "by changing the grammatical structure or by adding single words or phrases, usually adjectival."[26] In other words, Joyce sharpened the connection between the subheads and the text, joining them more tightly to that text while at the same time in no way diminishing their irony. This irony is particularly directed at the fuddy-duddiness of the professor in Stephen's company and soon (in "Scylla") at the aestheticism of the Dublin literary establishment. Stephen knows by this time that his art will not be like theirs. He will begin (like Joyce in *Dubliners*) by describing with little embellishment mean lives, and out of this meanness, this ordinariness, will come a beauty which the professor and the rest cannot know. Joyce's attitude toward aestheticism, though expressed differently, does not differ so markedly from Tzara's or the Dadaists' as one might expect. In addition, in other revisions of the "Aeolus" text as well as in the fundamental imagery of the episode, Joyce emphasizes one of the favorite devices of Dadaist imagery—one quite distinct either from Cubism or Futurism in its particular application— that of the machine.

Nelson's pillar and the tramlines mentioned in the episode were both added to the first *placards*. The second in particular increased the significance of the machine imagery, already prominent in the form of the printing presses, to Joyce's representation of the "heart" of the city. In Futurist work, the automobile and the locomotive were the most important machines, symbols of modern civilization sweeping past the debris of Western culture.[27] In Dadaist work, the machine imagery was less specific, but more integral to the total conception of the work; it was therefore perhaps an even better reflection of the significance of the machine in modern life. The work of Picabia illustrates this aspect of Dada art well. His *Picture Painted in Order to Tell, Not to Prove* (1915) (Figure 33)—a work which in fact anticipates, rather than directly reflects, the Dadaist program—resembles nothing more than a drawing of machine parts, cylinders at the heart of some undescribed whole, and is typical both of other work of Picabia of this period and of Dadaist work in general.[28] The tramlines and printing presses of "Aeolus" have a specific function important to their being in the episode, but to the extent that they symbolize modern civilization, they are related to the same sort of imagery in Dadaist art. Furthermore, Picabia's title anticipates Stephen's aesthetic as expressed in "Aeolus," his representation of "LIFE IN THE RAW."

Dadaist or Cubist collage, of course, is not the only possible source for the headlines and captions of "Aeolus." There are possible literary sources as well, but these are also closely connected with art movements. Apollinaire uses headlines, captions, and similar devices in his *Calligrammes* and other poetry in which spatial effects predominate, and these works are closely allied in intention and general aesthetic effect with the goals of Cubism.[29] Marinetti and the Futurists experimented with various typographical effects in poetry as well as in prose (indeed their work largely obliterates the distinction between the two), all in conjunction with the general Futurist program.[30] And Mallarmé, whose *Coup de dès* may be said to anticipate what Joyce does in "Aeolus" and whose work has obvious influence elsewhere on Joyce, was also a major influence on Apollinaire's generation and the one which preceded it in French poetry. The literary associations or antecedents which can be pointed to thus merely serve to reinforce the possibility of Cubist or Dadaist influence on Joyce, not to suggest some alternative to it.[31]

The headlines and captions of "Aeolus" represent an instance of the possible direct influence on Joyce's work by Cubism or its offshoots. The use of the fragment in *Ulysses* and in collage illustrates an instance of similarity of aesthetic purpose, if not of direct influence. This last point might also be made about the temporal-spatial relationships with which this consideration began. What remains is to see some general relationship between *Ulysses* and Cubism which touches not only on details of subject matter or technique, but also on the very essence of the art which each represents. That is in fact provided by what we might term the critical element in each, an element which raises fundamental questions about the nature of art at the same time that it criticizes by its very example all art which precedes it.

We have already noted, in reference to *Les Demoiselles d'Avignon*, the first major occurrence of a stylistic feature which was to characterize Cubism and Picasso's work in particular: the apposition in one field of elements which are temporally diverse or which represent different modes of rendering reality. All the major Cubists at one time or another experimented with such apposition, though Picasso perhaps carried it further than anyone else, stylistic diversity being an inherent feature of his artistic personality, not simply a *tour de force*. Individual works of others, however, may make plainer the aesthetic purpose of such deliberate diversity, for what it chiefly comes to in the end is the apposition of illusionistic and nonillusionistic devices—of techniques, that is, associated with, or derived from, the tradition of illusionism, dating back at least to the time of the Renaissance, and techniques associated with the departures, the *new* conventions as it were, of Cubism itself. This apposition creates a tension in much Cubist work which accounts in part for its aesthetic interest; it also constitutes a form of criticism built into the work of art, a graphic judgment of the various modes of rendering reality in aesthetic terms offered by the work itself. A collage by Juan Gris of 1914 provides a programmatic view of this matter.

In *The Table* (Figure 34) Gris juxtaposes two major elements—first, cut and pasted pieces of paper (including a fragment or two of newspaper) on which objects have been sketched in charcoal, occupying fully three-quarters of the picture surface and suggesting, with the lines that form an angle somewhere just below the bottom left of the canvas, a table top and its contents; and, second, at the lower right of the composition (even in this assembly an anachronism) a key casting a shadow. The pipe, the cigarettes, the bottles, the newspaper, and the book clearly suggest a traditional still-life arrangement, but disasssembled or rearranged to serve the purposes of the composition. The key suggests something else, to which the fragment of newspaper headline diagonally opposite to it provides the key. "LE VRAI ET LE FAUX" the headline begins, suggesting the real subject of the composition—two aesthetic choices not entirely resolved. The key casts a shadow, which suggests the illusionism of *trompe l'oeil,* from which such still life is generically derived. The remainder of the composition, which includes the headline, suggests the artistic freedom and essential two-dimensionality of Cubism, pictorially the opposite of *trompe l'oeil,* although related to it in subject matter. Which is the artistic reality of the composition? While it presents alternatives which can never be entirely resolved, Gris's composition obviously leans toward the freedom of form of Cubism. The oval shape, which fits perfectly into the rectangular confines of the composition and which suggests, with the complementary oval shape outlined in the top center, a palette, serves both to unify the diverse elements in the composition and to remind us symbolically that this unity is achieved in the end by the hand of the artist—his the shaping force behind the differing aesthetic visions. In composition, therefore, as well as in subject matter, *The Table* is at the center of the Cubist program and hence at the center of the modern artistic imagination, reshaping reality to suit its own purposes.

The fragment of a page of fiction toward the bottom of the composition reinforces the synthesis suggested in the whole. As the key which casts a shadow contrasts with the other still-life elements in the center, so this page of fiction represents a contrasting version of reality to that of the newspaper account. The "news" of the page of fiction and the "news" in the newspaper account may not be temporally diverse, but they surely represent alternative modes of truth, of rendering reality; the modes suggested by the nail and the still-life composition in the center of the canvas *are* temporally diverse, illusionism having been supplanted by the freer, more recent vision of the Cubists, which dominates the composition. This then becomes a form of criticism, a comment on the past as telling as Apollinaire's judgment, in "The Cubist Painters," that "Cubism differs from the old schools of painting in that it aims, not at an art of imitation, but at an art of conception, which tends to rise to the height of creation."[32] The same elements had appeared earlier in Cubist art—in pre-collage days—especially in the work of Braque. For example, his *Violin and Palette* (1909-10) (Figure 35) juxtaposes a nail casting a shadow with elements of a traditional still-life composition transformed.[33]

Futurism provides the same kind of comment on past art, but even more programmatically. Marinetti and the others connected with the movement agreed, in the "Manifesto of Futurism," that the literature of "pensive immobility, ecstasy, and sleep" was to be supplanted by the literature of "aggressive action, a feverish insomnia, the racer's stride, the mortal leap, the punch and the slap," and they also agreed that, in art, the automobile—in particular a racing car "whose hood is adorned with great pipes, like serpents of explosive breath"—was more beautiful than the *Victory of Samothrace*.[34] At the same time, however, Boccioni, the sculptor of the movement and probably its greatest artist, chooses to refer directly to the *Victory* in his *Unique Forms of Continuity in Space* (1913) (Figure 36), in his effort to revitalize the nude, by then officially regarded by the Futurists as having become an exhausted form. We must read Boccioni's form as not unique, but as part of the same commentary on the artistic tradition as that contained in the work of Gris and the Cubists—a criticism of Renaissance form. Futurist collage frequently achieves the same sort of contrast, as we can see, for instance, in Enrico Prampolini's *Spatial Rhythms* (1913),[35] where a title page from an edition of the *Divina Commedia* is juxtaposed with a fragment from a contemporary newspaper. These elements represent the same alternative modes to be seen in the Gris work of one year later. Similarly, Duchamp, in his irreverent and well-known parody of tradition in *"L.H.O.O.Q."* (1919) (Figure 37)—in many ways, like much of his work of the period, the very essence of Dada at the same time that it is uniquely Duchamp's—at once mocks parlor reproductions of art, the illusionistic tradition, and aestheticism in general. The joke, however, like that in much of Dada, depends upon a recognition of the tradition the Mona Lisa represents. In more recent work influenced by collage techniques, Robert Rauschenberg also frequently juxtaposes images from the past with images from the present to achieve ironic effect in his "combine paintings," as for example, in *Tracer* (1964),[36] in which a fragment from Rubens is juxtaposed with images of the eagle (as an American symbol) and a contemporary street scene.

Joyce presents the reader with similar choices, not entirely resolved, in *Ulysses*. "Cyclops" and "Aeolus" both represent an essentially spatial conception of form employing diverse temporal elements congruent with Cubist conceptions of time and space; they also give us alternative modes of narration which contrast markedly with the main narrative in much the same way that Gris's tabletop and key (or newspaper and novel fragments) contrast with each other. The 33 interpolated sections in "Cyclops" do not all contrast in time with the main narrative, but they most certainly do contrast in style and tone. They give us alternative renderings of the scene, contrasting the realistic, at times nearly self-parodying *patois* of the main narrative with the fabular and more modern styles, including the newspaper, of the interpolations. In "Aeolus" the same contrast is achieved with the headlines or captions, though in these the contrast is more in the nature of an aside than an alternative rendering of the scene. The contrast between the tone of the subheads of the episode and the main narrative suggests something of the tension which Stephen feels over his new subject matter. His art, by implication, is both an imitation of reality and a transcendence of that imitation, and the artist both maker and mocker. This contrast also suggests something essential to the technique of *Ulysses* as a whole, where so frequently, as in *The Table*, we are somewhere between two versions of reality. It is of the essence of Joyce's art in *Ulysses* that differing versions of reality not be completely resolved—that the truth, if in fact there is a truth, be a suspended one, held somewhere between Stephen's recalcitrance and Bloom's uncertainty, as in the closing pages of "Ithaca."

It is in "Oxen of the Sun," however, that Joyce achieves the maximum variety of styles in *Ulysses*, and it is here, in this episode in which the historical dimension is so obvious from the very beginning, that the relationship of *Ulysses* to the prose tradition becomes plainest. This relationship is to be seen by contrast with other portions of the novel—with the episodes before and after "Oxen"—rather than, as in "Cyclops" or "Aeolus," within the episode itself. Nonetheless, the styles of "Oxen" function as do the illusionistic references in Cubist work or the various references to artistic tradition in Futurist and Dadaist work—to remind us of where we have been as well as where we have arrived. Joyce deepens the irony of the contrast by ending with the screaming rhetoric of a twentieth-century revivalist, bellowing his message to the masses, but even this section of the episode is located clearly in time and has the aesthetic distinction of anticipating, in the pages just preceding it, the style of *Finnegans Wake*. The styles of "Oxen," like the general framework of *The Odyssey* to which Joyce adheres, serve to root *Ulysses* to the very traditions it most signally departs from, as Gris's key or the outline of the *Victory* or the page of Dante or the mustachioed upper lip of the *Mona Lisa* remind us, in the visual arts, of similar points of departure.

But the critical attitude implicit in this choice of styles is not limited in *Ulysses* or in the visual arts to a view of the past; both extend the same critical attitude toward themselves, passing their own innovations through the same process of judgment. In the earliest phase of Cubist art, as the object is gradually "destroyed" and reassembled in the form of flat planes on the picture surface, the object all but disappears and, with it, color and almost all attempts at creating the illusion of depth, the long-cherished third dimension. Cubist painting, exploring new dimensions of space, thus sacrifices the most fundamental spatial illusion of all. With the development of collage, however, new textures and colors enter into Cubist art, as well as more simplified renderings of forms. These textures, color, and forms provide comment on the "real" world, but they also comment on the newly established world of Cubist art, of which they are both an extension and a criticism. They occur as much in response to those freely formed fields of shifting planes from the analytical phase, as they do to the more traditional shapes and forms of *trompe l'oeil*.

This tendency toward self-criticism in the Cubist movement entered a third phase in the period just prior to the outbreak of World War I, when the techniques of collage—which represented a logical development aesthetically from the earlier, analytical phase of Cubism—began to be simulated in paintings and collages in which one is not certain which elements are collage and which are not. In this Platonic process, in which copies are made form copies, we are not certain, at least at first glance, what is copied and what is not. These works also use color more freely than their predecessors do, and often suggest some sense of depth. The whole movement of Cubism, then, is essentially one from fragmentation to synthesis, a full circle in which the Cubists end by criticizing their own achievement as thoroughly as they do that of any movements or individual artists who preceded them.

We can see this development only by surveying the whole of Cubist art and its related movements from the beginnings to 1914, in as nearly chronological order as can be achieved. However, as with so many of the other major features of Cubist style, Picasso's work in itself provides examples of precisely this kind of synthesis. In a number of works from a somewhat later period, at the very end of the war, as if in an attempt to review the Cubist achievement at the time the world of art had entered into a major period of transition, Picasso explicitly explores the relationship between Cubism and the illusionistic tradition and hence the progress of his own work up to that time. The most striking instance of this exploration comes perhaps in *The Window* (1919) (Figure 38), where a Cubist still life appears on a table in front of a balcony giving a view of sky and sea. The suggestion in the scene of the classical window on the world in plain, and so is the contrast between the Cubist treatment of the table and its objects and the more traditional treatment of the space behind and beyond them. As if to comment on the balance of past and present which the painting represents— the individual talent balanced against the tradition, the Cubist achievement balanced against the classical perspective, and Picasso's current work compared with his earlier—the shadow lines in the lower foreground, which would pull the spectator's eye through the grating to the sea in the middle distance, are cut off at the very edge of the picture by a collage-like cut-out which represents the folds of the tablecloth. It is difficult to find a clearer instance of one of the fundamental sources of tension in Cubist art, nor a better instance of Picasso's awareness of his own aesthetic heritage—the subject being, in the well-known phrase of Meyer Shapiro's, the *possibilities* of painting.[37]

This phenomenon—of the artist self-consciously recapitulating his own achievement in a single work or a short series of works—is in fact typical of the history of avant-garde art. Duchamp's work provides a similar instance in *Tu m'* (1918) (Figure 39), a large work which sums up all that precedes it and represents Duchamp's farewell to painting, a form to which he never returned after this time. The summation occurs by reference to the styles of his preceding works in this medium, as well as to specific images from that work. The work of more recent artists such as Rauschenberg, Robert Motherwell, and Jasper Johns continues the phenomenon, which depends both upon a high degree of self-consciousness and upon a variety of styles or subjects from one hand.

Ulysses is in the same sense an act of self-criticism, a summation of Joyce's previous achievement in fiction and a criticism of itself. We have already noted in discussing the use of the fragment the stylistic relationship to *A Portrait*. In ways still myriad after more than sixty years, the styles of *Ulysses*—of Stephen's episodes especially—may be said to grow out of Joyce's first novel, defining Stephen's character and psyche through ironic interplay among subject, theme, and prose style. In the same sense, through Stephen's decision in "Aeolus" to write of "dear dirty Dublin" and the virgins of Fumbally Lane,

Joyce treats ironically the style of his very first work of prose fiction—the style of *Dubliners*—in the context of Stephen's emerging aesthetic.

Beyond this, however, Joyce turns on his own achievement in *Ulysses*, subjecting it to the same sort of critical view and hence, to some degree at least, the same sort of irony. If the book begins in a style which grows out of that of *A Portrait*, and appropriately enough with a character with whom we have become familiar there, we soon enough become aware that we are in a different narrative mode. With the introduction of the phrase "As he and others see me" (*U* 6.28) (a phrase which is anticipated by the otherwise enigmatic "Chrysostomos" of 3.28), as Stephen looks at himself in Buck Mulligan's mirror, we realize that a new dimension of narrative is being opened to us, one which the succeeding pages develop and, increasingly, depend on. By the early episodes with Bloom, this technique, a few incongruities aside, has become firmly established and has begun to give the reader the pleasure that comes with recognition. However, this recognition is no sooner established than Joyce begins to shift ground, to move in the new directions of the later episodes of the book. With "Aeolus" and then "Scylla" (taking the episodes as they occur in the final text and not as they were actually written) the stream technique so firmly established in the earlier episodes of the book is subjected to increasing degrees of irony by the introduction of new voices in the narrative—voices which mock and question the subjective intimacies which the stream technique provides. The headlines and captions of "Aeolus" provide many instances of such ironies. Similarly, it is significant that in "Scylla," when the narrative takes on the form of the subject of the episode, which is drama, it does so immediately before or after sections written from Stephen's more subjective point of view. Thus, on 203, where the iambic pentameter suggests the style of Elizabethan drama, a stream passage follows, from Stephen's point of view, after *"Punkt"* (*U* 203.25-30), and at 208.42, after Stephen's thought "Come mess," the whole section of dialogue on 209 takes the specific form of drama, in anticipation of the later "Circe." It is as if Joyce had tired of his own creation and felt the necessity to vary it as soon as it had become established in the reader's mind. By the later episodes—"Oxen" for example—the stream technique is all but buried beneath the layers of alternative techniques and styles. The final word comes perhaps with "Penelope," where Joyce provides what is in some respects the most subjective episode of all. At the same time, however, Joyce, like Picasso and other major figures of the avant-garde, seems constantly to need to question his own aesthetic means, to subject them to a form of self-criticism which is peculiarly modern, to move, in one work, beyond a style of his own creation.

One effect of this process upon the reader is to force him to become a part of the creative process itself. "By juxtaposing mimetic and abstract elements," notes Jessica Prinz Pecorino in an essay on Pound's work and the visual arts, Cubist painting or collage "expresses a dynamic interplay between visual data and the conceptualizing mind."[38] That is, the aesthetic interest of Cubist art lies not so much in the discerning of the object, figure, or set of associations which is the subject of the work as in the discerning or appreciating of the *process* by which that object, figure, or set of associations is created. In a sense, then, although the Cubists never abandoned the object, the subject of their art is the process of art itself. *Ulysses* also creates a tension between process and subject, style and substance, its art a delicate and always changing balance between the data of narrative and the various techniques by which that data may be rendered. The reader of *Ulysses,* like the spectator before the Cubist canvas, may never resolve this aesthetic tension, but in the act of perceiving it, in recognizing the process by which the work is created—by which the work in fact *exists*—he enters into it as fully as he can, on an imaginative level comparable to that of the artist himself.

The qualities of *Ulysses* thus far discussed as Cubist, or at any rate as related to the Cubist achievement in its various manifestations, are not peculiar to *Ulysses* alone. They also characterize other modern works of similar stature. Of particular interest in this regard, because of its long and close association with *Ulysses,* is *The Waste Land.*[39] There is, of course, no attempt in Eliot's poem to develop a continuous narrative in the manner of *Ulysses,* with one set of characters carrying story line and theme, but—that fundamental difference between the two literary works aside—the achievement of Eliot compares closely with that of Joyce in respect to Cubist aesthetic principles.

Like *Ulysses,* and like Cubist art, *The Waste Land* depends heavily upon the apposition of diverse temporal and spatial elements, with rapid shifts of time and place occurring in all parts of the poem except II and IV. Even in these sections, however, the same principle obtains. "A Game of Chess" depends for its effect, thematic and stylistic, upon the contrast between one space, with its associated voices, and another: the drawing room of exotic description, with the painting of Philomel over the mantel (77-110), in contrast with the lower-class pub and its "Aeolus"-like phrase "HURRY UP PLEASE ITS TIME" (139-172). There is also a strong suggestion in section II of a contrast in time. "Death by Water" in itself suggests no such contrasts but does support the general sense of temporal-spatial diversity characteristic of the whole work. In the other sections of the poem free movement in time and space, within a tight thematic framework, is of the very essence of Eliot's achievement.

Like *Ulysses* again, and like Cubist art, *The Waste Land* is frequently built of small syntactical units—fragments which, taken together, carry larger meanings. These fragments in Eliot's poem perhaps owe less to popular culture than they do in *Ulysses* or Cubism (though the imagery associated with Stephen in "Proteus," "Scylla" and elsewhere is by no means popular), but they are no less urban in their reference. As in the reading of *Ulysses,* the meaning of the fragments in *The Waste Land* is created by our reading of the poem as a whole, each section contributing to our sense of their final significance. We also find in the poem the same machine imagery to be found in "Aeolus," most notably in the reference to "The sound of horns and motors" (198) and the image of the human engine waiting (216-17). The effect of this imagery is the same as in "Aeolus": to suggest, as in Dada and Futurist art, the pervasive influence of the machine in modern life.

Like *Ulysses* still again, and like Cubist art, *The Waste Land* presents us in one work with a variety of styles. These styles are appropriate to particular voices or points of view and represent different ways of perceiving reality— views differing in terms of social class, historical perspective, and degree of aesthetic sensitivity. If there is no section of the poem which achieves the same historical view of literary style as "Oxen" does in *Ulysses*, there is still much that corresponds to the stylistic variety of *Ulysses*. The contrast of tones in "A Game of Chess," ending with the limited vocabulary and sensibility of the lower classes; the implied criticism of Romantic subjectivism in the opening lines of the poem, the private voice giving way to the public and in effect repudiating, or at least questioning, it—these and other elements of *The Waste Land* provide the same kind of historical (or social) criticism that we find in Joyce. We do not find, however, an extension of this critical attitude toward *The Waste Land* itself, Eliot subjecting his own achievement to criticism in the same sense that Joyce ends by criticizing his, though the ending of the poem, by alluding to the fragments "shored against my ruins" (431), does suggest that whatever order is achieved earlier is illusory.

In any event, there are a sufficient number of similarities between Eliot's achievement and Joyce's, in comparison with that of the Cubists, to say that Cubist aesthetic principles apply both to *The Waste Land* and to *Ulysses*. The work of Pound also illustrates these principles and, furthermore, has the improvisatory quality which the best of Cubist art frequently exemplifies, but the pursuit of these correspondences would take us into another country indeed. It is enough to say that if Cubism had relatively few major literary figures in its midst at the time it was conceived, it soon found many adherents to its principles—even those, like Joyce, to whom modern art was something of an anathema.

Futurism poses a slightly different case. For one thing, there was little in the Futurist program inherently attractive to Joyce. Futurist painting was at the same time abstract and literal—abstract in its imagery, yet literal in its titles and at times almost didactic in the way it attempted to carry out the ideas contained in the various Futurist manifestoes. On the other hand, Futurist poetry—like that of the Dadaists which followed it—was often devoid of sense, consisting of patterns of sounds which were at best only randomly suggestive of the Futurist philosophy. In short, both Futurist painting and Futurist poetry went against virtually all the traditions which Joyce's work upheld. If Joyce could have found pleasure, or even a certain inspiration, in the aesthetic experimentation of the Cubists—at once, like his own art in *Ulysses,* intellectually playful and emotionally contained—one can easily see why he would have found quite the opposite in the more strident work of the Futurists.[40]

However, in spite of the obvious differences in intentions and results between the efforts of the Futurists and the achievements of Joyce, several areas of similarity between his work and theirs have already been noted, notably in the use of machine imagery in "Aeolus" and in the use of classical antecedents to define the work of art. One may argue that the second of these is characteristic in one way or another of all Western art in all periods since classical times, present no less in the work of those who eschew the past than in the work of those who emulate it. One must see the first, however, as a particular contribution of Futurism to modern art and hence a link between Joyce's work and the Italian movement, although his machine imagery is in the end closer to that of the Dadaists. An even more important contribution of the Futurists than the imagery of the machine—and one to be seen elsewhere in *Ulysses*—is the dynamism which was at the core of the Futurist program and which formed the subject of so much of their art.

"Time and space died yesterday. We already live in the absolute, because we have created eternal, omnipresent speed"[41]—this and other portions of the general Futurist manifesto extolling the virtues of aggressiveness, energy, and speed found expression in work the very titles of which suggest the importance of the concept to the Futurist vision. Russolo's *Speeding Train* (1911), Balla's *Dynamism of a Dog Leash* (1912) and *Study for the Materiality of Lights plus Speed* (1913), as well as many other works, embody this dynamic principle, bringing it to life by color, line, and repetition of forms. Balla's work of 1913 (Figure 40) illustrates all of these elements, but particularly the effect of line and repeated forms in suggesting the dynamism which the Futurists cherished. The speeding trains or automobiles of earlier Futurist work give way here to more abstract forms, suggesting not just the motion of a particular object, but the act of motion itself.

The work of Wyndham Lewis and the English Vorticists—influenced in this respect by the Futurists—provides plentiful examples of the same phenomenon,[42] as well as the work of the Russian Futurists, such as Kasimir Malevich's *Knife-Grinder* (1912), which was also influenced by Italian Futurist work.[43] Marcel Duchamp's celebrated *Nude Descending a Staircase, No. 2* (1912), though apparently not influenced by Italian Futurism, reflects the same aesthetic intentions.[44] All of this work one way or another suggests the kinds of retinal after-images described in the "Technical Manifesto of Futurist Painting" of 1910:

> The gesture which we would reproduce on canvas shall no longer be a fixed *moment* in universal dynamism. It shall be the *dynamic sensation* itself.

> Indeed, all things move, all things run, all things are rapidly changing. A profile is never motionless before our eyes, but it constantly appears and disappears. On account of the persistency of an image upon the retina, moving objects constantly multiply themselves; their form changes like rapid vibrations, in their mad career. Thus a running horse has not four legs, but twenty, and their movements are triangular.[45]

The effect of such painting is, at its most literal, cinematographic—a depiction of successive movements of a figure or object in a limited field of space, the slightly varied forms of hands or feet or wheels suggesting the after-images of film or human visual perception itself. Unlike Cubist work of the same period, which had moved far beyond the literal representation of figures and objects to a shorthand of lines and planes which approached the abstract, this work often has a stronger narrative than plastic element to it. As William Rubin comments on Duchamp's *Nude,* "Its novel element—the 'representation' of movement by the depiction, in one picture, of successive phases of an object in movement— was a *narrative,* not a *plastic* innovation, and it did not open a new direction for painting."[46] Later Futurist work in this vein, however—as exemplified by Balla's *Study* (Figure 40)—is in fact far less literal in its subject matter than Duchamp's work, and therefore less narrative in its thrust.

In *Ulysses* the application of the same aesthetic principle is tied to specific figures, objects, or actions, but is never merely a literal representation of successive phases of movement. It was scarcely necessary for Joyce or any other novelist of innovative persuasion in his time to seek new means to represent successive motion in narrative form, since prose narrative by its very nature readily provides the means for such representation. One word, phrase, or sentence follows another, with the result that the chronological depiction of movement through space is easily achieved. At the same time, however, Joyce's variations on traditional modes of representing such successive motion suggest the same sensitivity to *"dynamic sensation"* that Futurist work provides.

The pace of the prose at that point in "Calypso" when Bloom realizes that the kidney is burning illustrates well a representation of an accelerated activity in normal consecutive order:

> He fitted the book roughly into his inner pocket and, stubbing his toes against the broken commode, hurried out towards the smell, stepping hastily down the stairs with a flurried stork's legs. Pungent smoke shot up in an angry jet from a side of the pan. By prodding a prong of the fork under the kidney he detached it and turned it turtle on its back. Only a little burned. He tossed it off the pan onto a plate and let the scanty brown gravy trickle over it. (*U* 65.26)

In "Nestor," when Stephen reads over the text of Mr. Deasy's letter to the editor, it is by means of a highly selective succession of phrases that his scanning is represented:

> Foot and mouth disease. Known as Koch's preparation. Serum and virus. Percentage of salted horses. Rinderpest. Emperor's horses at Mürzsteg, lower Austria. Veterinary surgeons. Mr. Henry Blackwood Price. Courteous offer a fair trial. Dictates of common sense. Allimportant question. In every sense of the word take the bull by the horns. Thanking you for the hospitality of your columns. (*U* 33.11)

In this paragraph and the one shortly preceding it we see Stephen's scanning of the text, each phrase retained in his memory only until succeeded by another. This is at once a literal representation of the act of perception and, in narrative terms, a figurative mode of representing a text. Like Futurist and Futurist-influenced art, it suggests by a succession of phrases or images the dynamic of perception itself. Similar examples—outgrowths or extensions of the technique of stream-of-consciousness—occur elsewhere in the text, for instance in "Calypso" when Bloom scans the letter from Milly (62.35) or later, in "Hades" (91.19) when, again, he scans the obituaries.[47]

In "Lotus-Eaters" another sort of vision based on moving images comparable to those of Futurist art occurs in the scene with Bloom and McCoy, as Bloom tries to catch a glimpse of stocking in front of the Grosvenor across the way: "Flicker, flicker: the lace flare of her hat in the sun: flicker, flick" (74.37). The tram passes away, like an image in a silent film or a Futurist canvas, reduced to a succession of shimmering, vibrating planes. Furthermore, in precisely the manner of the lines of motion in Futurist painting, the carriage moves across Bloom's field of vision from right to left. If the tendency of Joyce's technique elswhere in *Ulysses* is to reduce figures and objects, in the manner of Cubism, to a single, often fragmented, characteristic (even in this very passage, as in line 27: "Silk flash rich stockings white"), here the image is repetitive and transient in keeping both with the subject and with Bloom's perception of it.

Dada would also seem to have relatively little in common with Joyce's achievement in *Ulysses,* beyond the analogies already cited. Joyce's anti-aestheticism was limited largely to pokes at themes or styles associated with the Dublin literati of the period of the 1890s and the turn of the century, including the view of the artist which was general then.[48] This parodic aspect of his art, however, was subordinate in *Ulysses* to the more important desire to create the beautiful from the ordinary, and history from the moment. The Dadaists were savagely committed to the destruction of all known principles of art, including many that Joyce personally prized greatly. Their goal in fact was not art at all, but anti-art, and their use of tradition was far overshadowed by their abuse of it. At the same time, however, their work was also capable of imbuing ordinary objects with qualities usually associated with works of art, and therefore they managed, like Joyce, to create the beautiful from the ordinary.

Duchamp in particular was successful in taking utilitarian objects—bicycle wheels or douches—and turning them into objects of mysterious beauty which set a whole trend in twentieth-century art. These objects, which he termed "ready-mades," are displayed in such a way as to be dissociated from their normal functions, but they are identifiable both as functional objects (what they were) and objects of art (what, by being so displayed, they have become).[49] As in *Ulysses*, where ordinary objects and events are constantly being elevated to a level of artistic significance, these objects, at once so homely and yet so aesthetically right, provide their own alternative to the conventional subjects of art and to the heroic tradition these subjects frequently suggest. The emphasis on the ordinary or trivial begun with Impressionism comes to its final fruition in these objects of Duchamp's.

For the Dadaist the artistic intention is more important than the artistic result, and the artistic act a happy accident, not a calculated plan. For Joyce the result is always more important than the intention, and the art almost never accidental, but increasingly, as he went on with *Ulysses* and then to the earliest stages of "Work in Progress," the emphasis of his work is on the process of language and the possibilities of narrative rather than upon particular characters or completed events. As single meanings gave way to multiple, and one vision of an event to another, traditional modes of narration and signification were amplified, inverted, or destroyed; all was cast in doubt, as, in the words of Adaline Glasheen, Joyce "put his artist's money on the dark horse Incertitude."[50] For him, as for the Dadaists, their successors the Surrealists, and all the other avant-garde artists, the process of art became at least as important as its results, and, the form of the work of art, as in the best of modern art, inextricably entwined, in the classic formulation, with its increasingly complicated function.

Illustrations

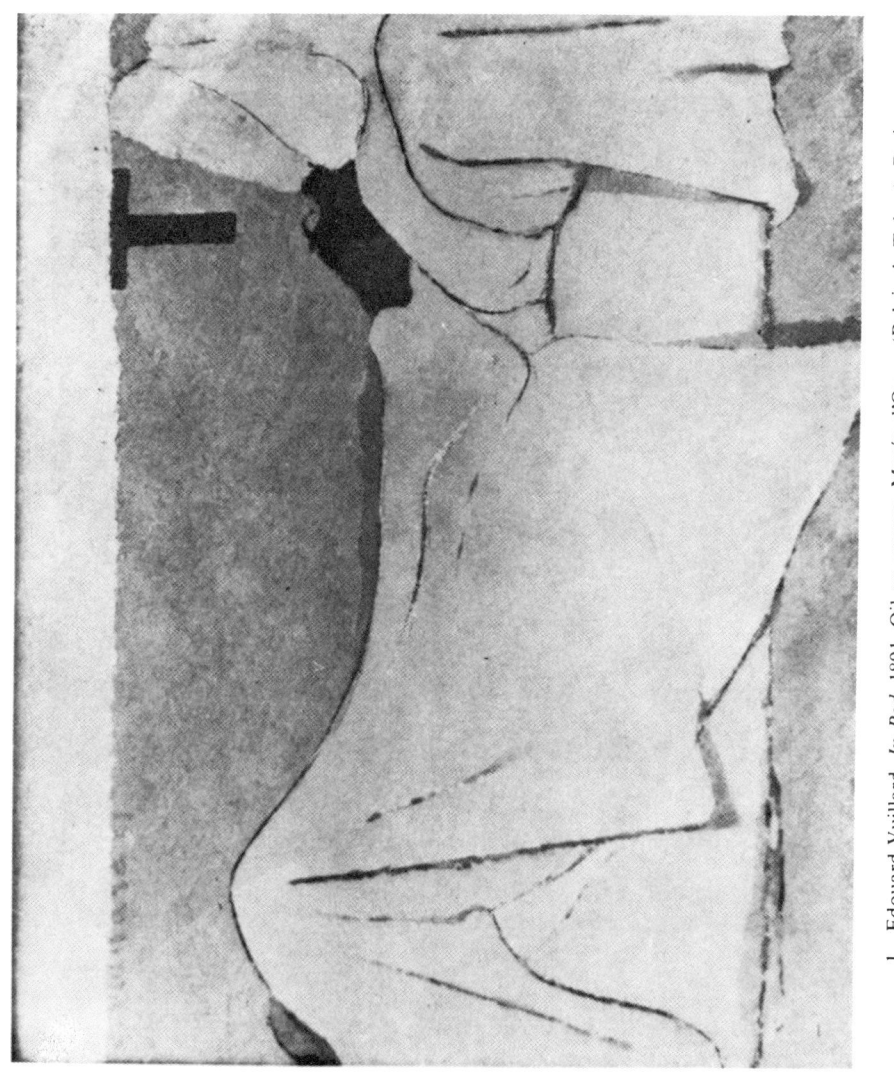

1. Edouard Vuillard. *In Bed*. 1891. Oil on canvas. Musée d'Orsay (Palais de Tokyo), Paris

2. Edouard Vuillard. *Mystery.* c. 1895. Oil on board. Private collection, New York

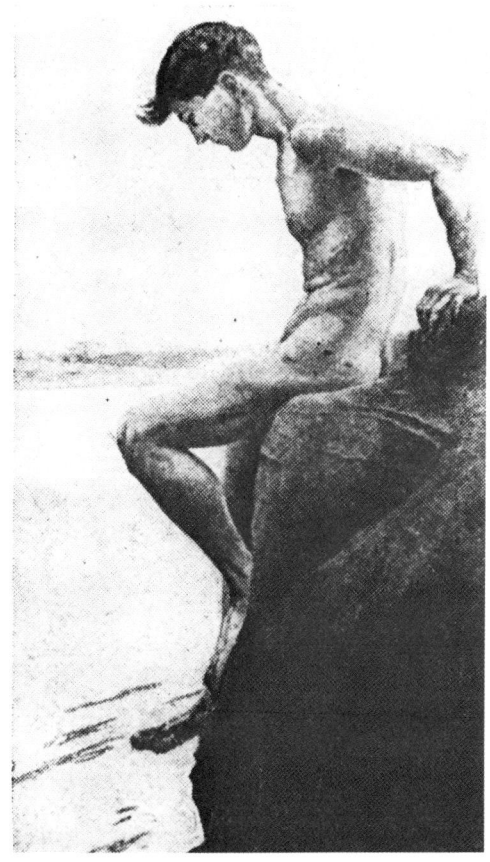

3. Roberto Basilici. *On the Tiber*. c. 1900-1910. Present whereabouts unknown

4. Aristide Maillol. Illustration to Virgil's *Eclogues*. (Published Weimar: Cranach Press, 1925)

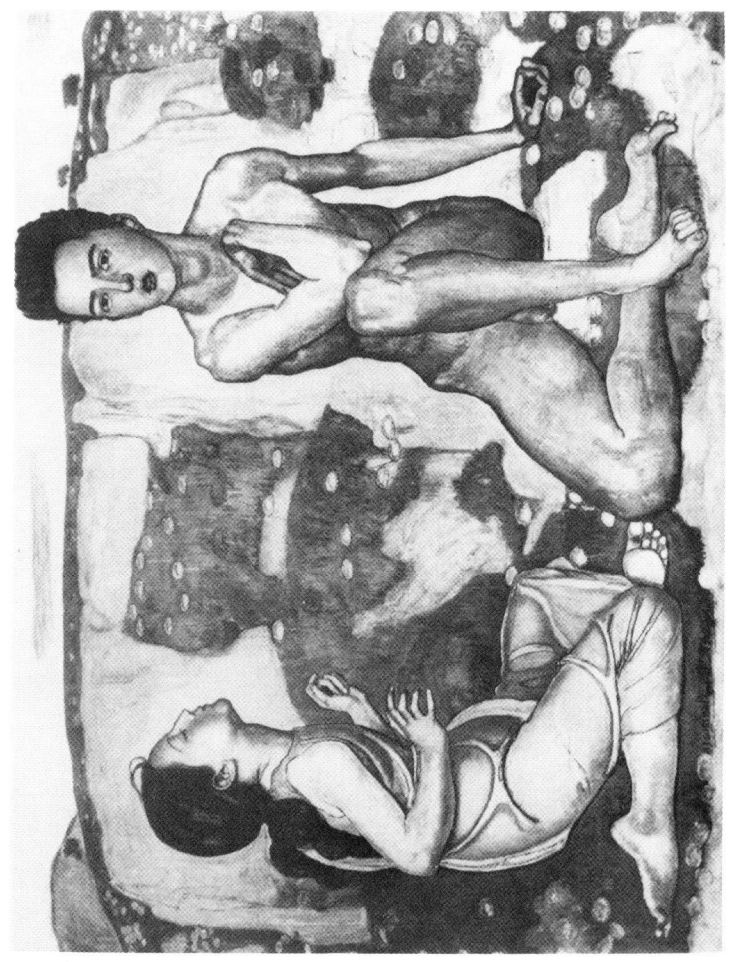

5. Ferdinand Hodler. *Spring*. 1901. Oil. Museum Folkwang, Essen

6. Ferdinand Hodler. *Youth Admired by Women*. 1903. Oil. Kunsthaus Zürich (on loan from the Gottfied Keller Foundation)

7. Ferdinand Hodler. *Distant View*. 1906. Oil. Present whereabouts unknown

8. Edvard Munch. *Melancholy*. 1901. Color woodcut. Munch Museum, Oslo

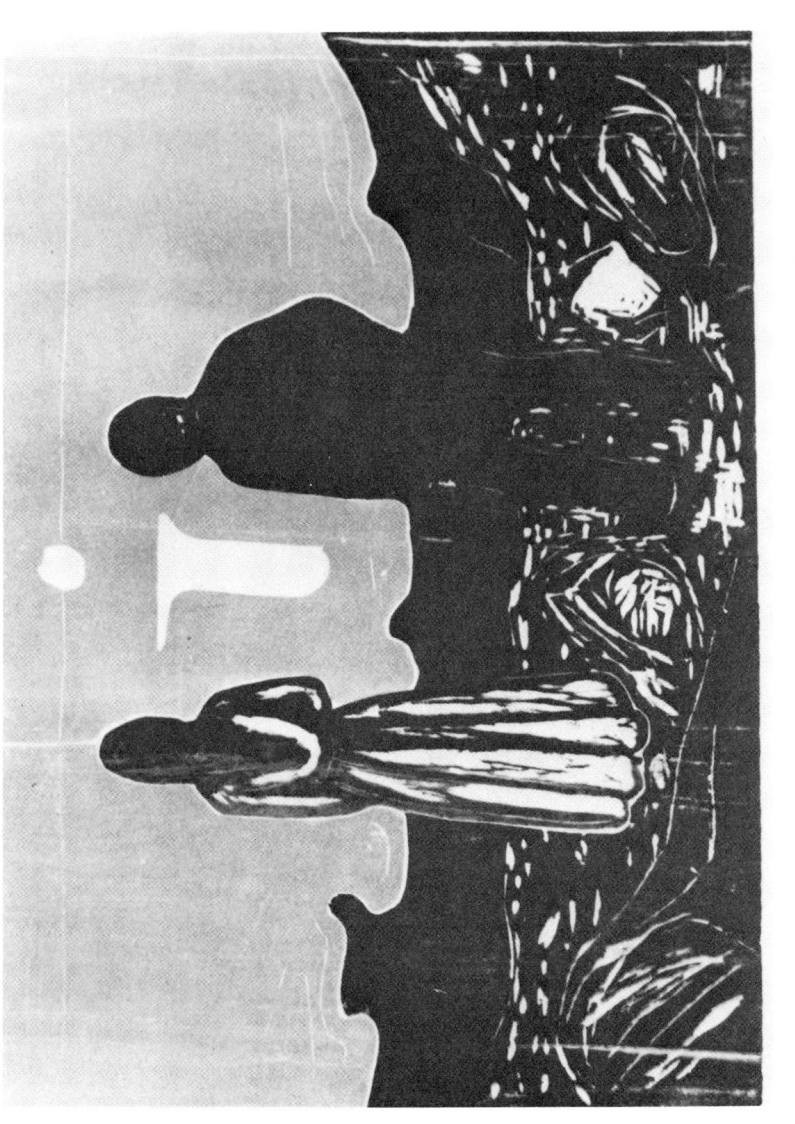

9. Edvard Munch. *The Lonely Ones.* 1899. Color woodcut. Munch Museum, Oslo

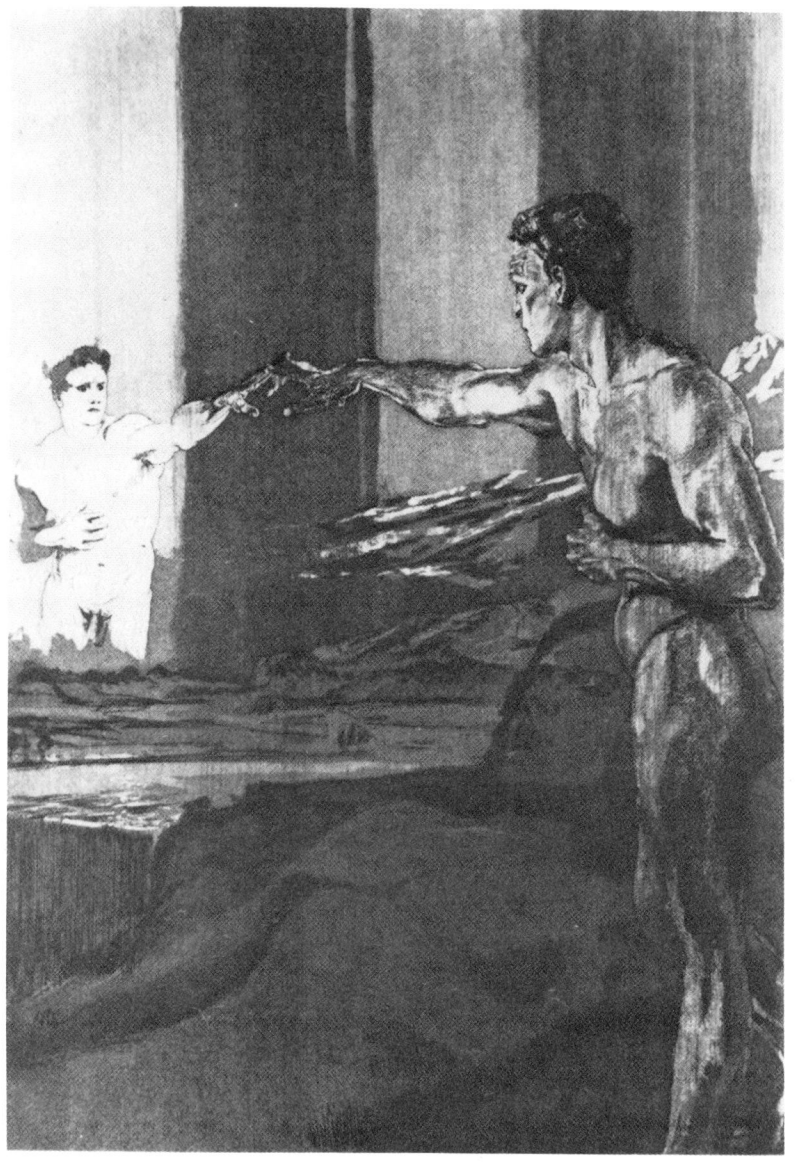

10. Max Klinger. *The Philosopher*. 1910. Etching. Staatliche Graphische Sammlung, Munich

11. Emile Bernard. *Self-Portrait (Vision)*. 1891. Oil. Present whereabouts unknown

12. Meyer de Haan. *Self-Portrait*. 1890. Oil. Present whereabouts unknown

13. Paul Gauguin. *Te Po (The Great Night)*. 1894. Woodcut. (First published in 1921)

14. Edvard Munch. *Death in the Sickroom.* 1895. Oil. Munch Museum, Oslo

15. Rudolf Jettmar. *The Poet*. Etching. Present whereabouts unknown

16. Alphonse Mucha. Printed velvet design. c. 1900.

17. Robert Burns. *Natura Naturans.* 1891

18. Dante Gabriel Rossetti. *Astarte Syriaca*. c. 1867. Drawing. Present whereabouts unknown

19. Odilon Redon. *Closed Eyes.* 1890. Musée d'Orsay (Palais de Tokyo), Paris

20. Edvard Munch. Madonna. 1895. Color lithograph. Munch Museum, Oslo

21. Paul Gauguin. *Breton Eve.* 1889. Pastel and aquarelle. Marion Koogler McNay Art Museum, San Antonio

22. Edvard Munch. *Man's Head in Woman's Hair*. 1896. Color woodcut. Munch Museum, Oslo

23. Gustave Moreau. *Apparition.* Cabinet des Dessins, Musée du Louvre, Paris

24. Edvard Munch. *Woman*. 1899. Color lithograph. Munch Museum, Oslo

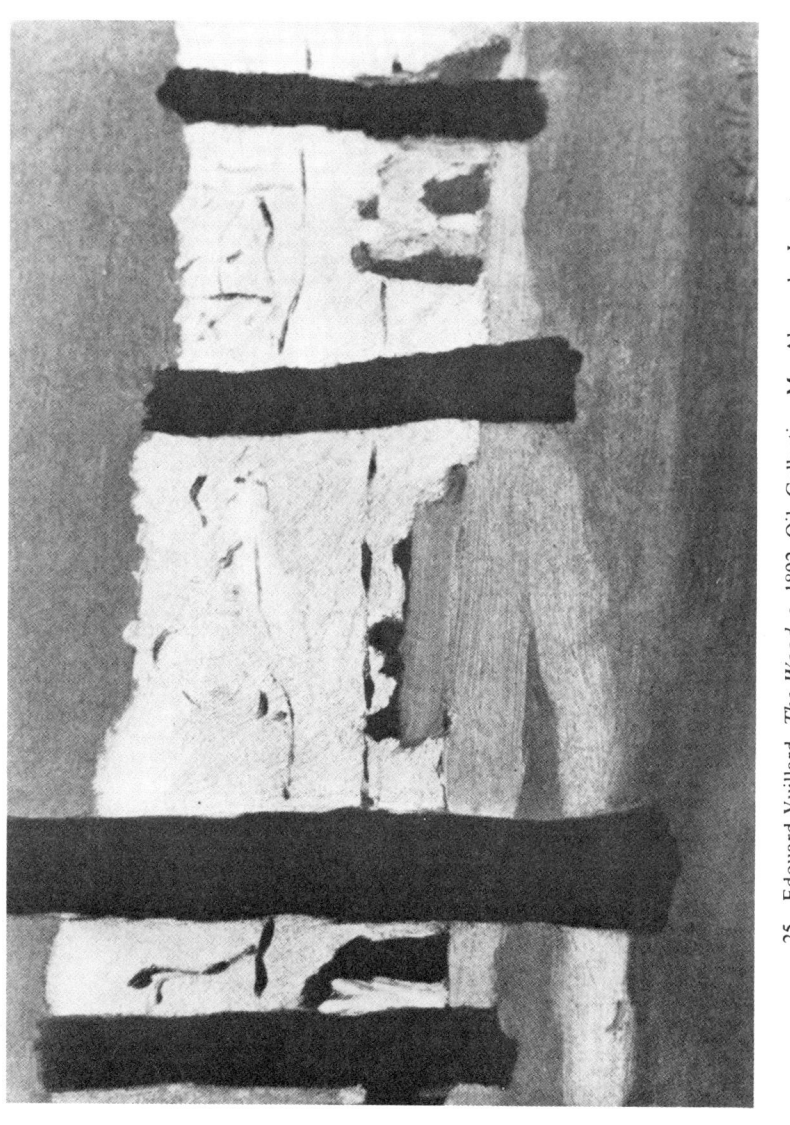

25. Edouard Vuillard. *The Wood.* c. 1892. Oil. Collection Mr. Alexander Lewyt

26. Paul Sérusier. *Incantation*. 1890. Oil. Present whereabouts unknown

27. Edvard Munch. *The Voice*. 1893. Oil on canvas. Museum of Fine Arts, Boston

28. Moritz von Schwind. *The Organic Life of Nature (Das Organische Leben der Natur)*. Drawing

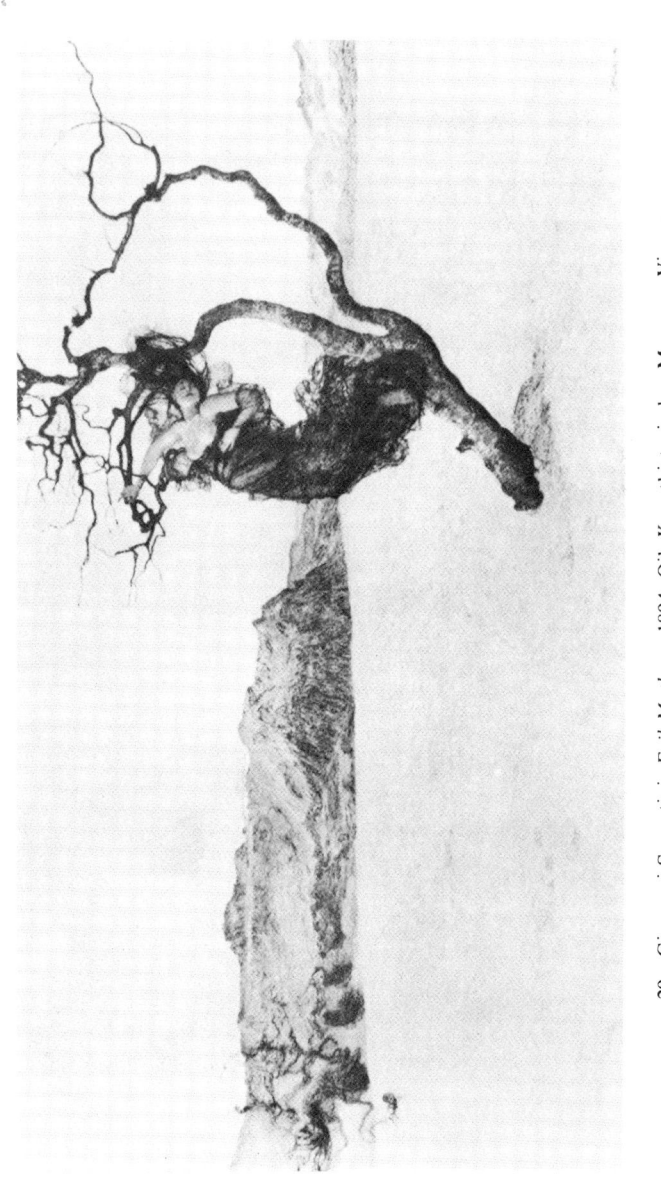

29. Giovanni Segantini. *Evil Mothers*. 1894. Oil. Kunsthistorisches Museum, Vienna

30. Albert Weigerber. *Reclining Figure in a Mountainous Landscape.* 1914. Staatsgalerie moderner Kunst, Munich

31. Edvard Munch. *Winter*. 1899. Oil. Munch Museum, Oslo

32. Pablo Picasso. *Les Demoiselles d'Avignon.* 1907. Oil on canvas. The Museum of Modern Art, New York (Acquired through the Lillie P. Bliss Bequest)

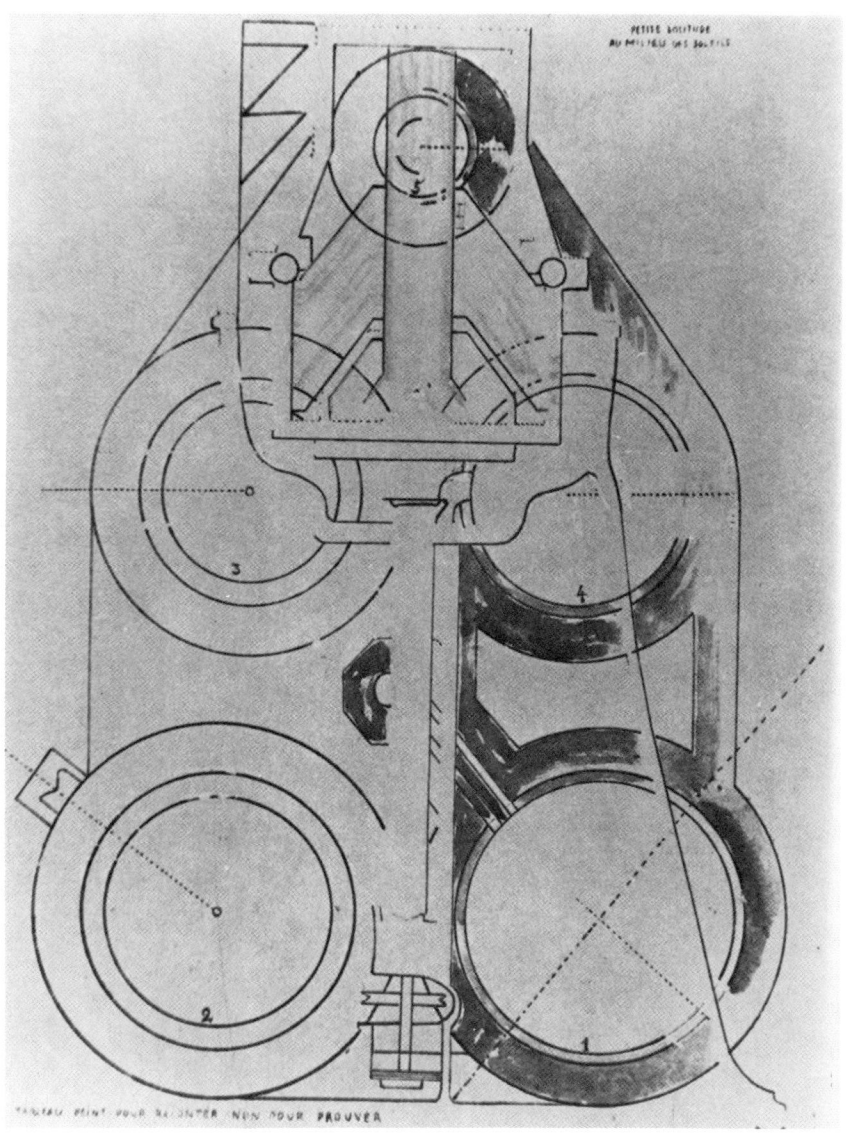

33. Francis Picabia. *Picture Painted in order to Tell, not to Prove*. 1915. Pen and ink and gouache on tracing paper. Present whereabouts unknown

34. Juan Gris. *The Table*. 1914. Collage on canvas. Philadelphia Museum of Art

35. Georges Braque. *Violin and Palette.* 1909-10. Oil on canvas. The Solomon R. Guggenheim Museum, New York

36. Umberto Boccioni. *Unique Forms of Continuity in Space.* 1913. Bronze. The Museum of Modern Art, New York (Acquired through the Lillie P. Bliss Bequest)

37. Marcel Duchamp. *L.H.O.O.Q.* 1919. Reproduction, altered by pencil. Private collection

38. Pablo Picasso. *The Window*. 1919. Gouache. Private collection

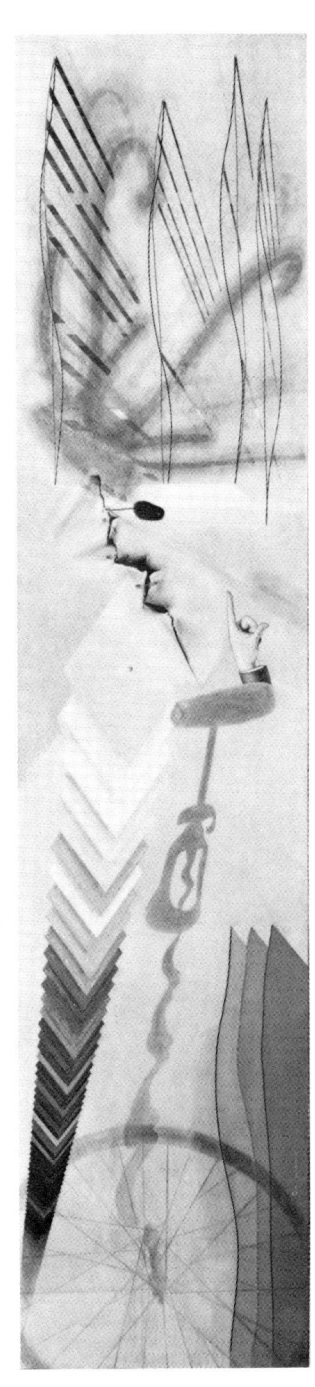

39. Marcel Duchamp. *Tu m'*. 1918. Oil and graphite on canvas (with objects). Yale University Art Gallery (Bequest of Katherine S. Dreier)

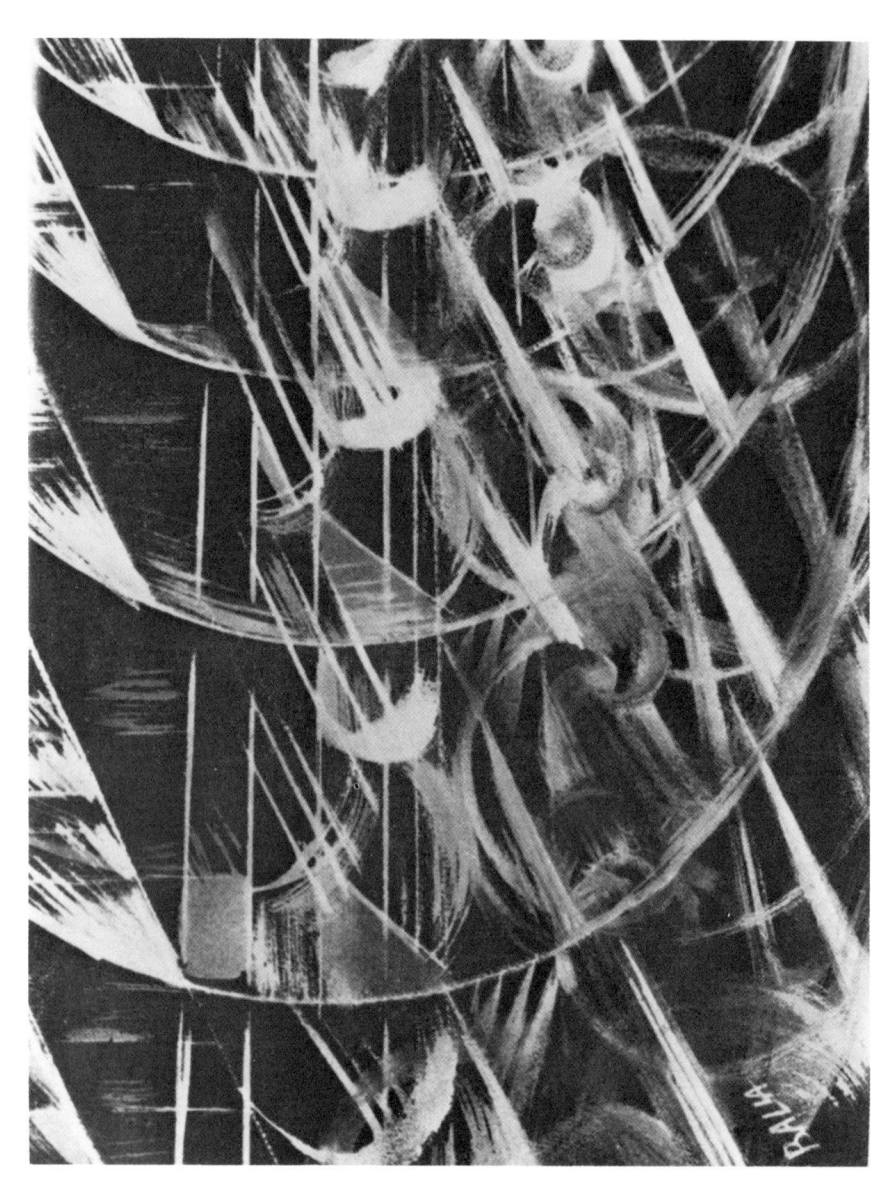

40. Giacomo Ball. *Study for the Materiality of Lights plus Speed.* 1913. Gouache. Collection Lydia Winston Malbin

Notes

Chapter 1

1. *The Workshop of Daedalus: James Joyce and the Raw Materials for* A Portrait of the Artist as a Young Man, coll. and ed. Robert Scholes and Richard M. Kain (Evanston, IL: Northwestern University Press, 1965), p. 83, hereafter *WDaed.*

2. *WDaed,* p. 96. Maria Elisabeth Kronegger's *James Joyce and Associated Image Makers* (New Haven: College and University Press, 1968) is the only other book-length study of Joyce's imagery and technique in relationship to the visual arts.

3. All references to *A Portrait of the Artist as a Young Man* are to the Viking Compass text of 1964, hereafter *P.*

4. All references to *Dubliners* are to the Viking Compass text of 1967, hereafter *D.*

5. The reference to Shelley in the quoted passage is significant in terms of Stephen's fledgling status as an artist. The Shelleyan references in *A Portrait,* as Wylie Sypher points out in "Portrait of the Artist as John Keats," *Virginia Quarterly Review,* 25 (1949), pp. 420-28, connote the preoccupation with self that prevents Stephen from becoming an artist. The paragraph that follows in *A Portrait*—beginning "The dull light fell more faintly" (*P* 103)— suggests the escape from self which begins for Stephen at the conclusion of the novel. Taken together, the two paragraphs come close to representing a paradigm of Stephen's development in the novel as a whole. Cf. Richard Ellmann, *James Joyce,* new and rev. ed. (New York: Oxford University Press, 1982), pp. 295-99.

6. *The Early Work of Aubrey Beardsley* (New York: Da Capo Press, 1967), pl. 143.

7. Ibid., pl's. 150 and 151.

8. According to Leslie Hancock, *Word Index to James Joyce's* Portrait of the Artist (Carbondale: Southern Illinois University Press, 1967).

9. On this subject, see Maurice Beebe, *Ivory Towers and Sacred Founts: The Artist as Hero in Fiction from Goethe to Joyce* (New York: New York University Press, 1964), esp. p. 266 ff.

10. On Nabi art and symbolism, see George Mauner, *The Nabis: Their History and Their Art, 1888-1896* (New York: Garland Publishers, 1978).

11. I realize that in separating image and technique I am committing what some will regard as a fatal critical error, but I do not see how, for purposes of this discussion, I can proceed otherwise. Like many distinctions, it seems to me, it is artificial, but necessary. If the term "technique" is vague, I can only hope that the following commentary will make its various meanings plainer.

12. By Kronegger, and also by Maurice Beebe, "The *Portrait* as Portrait: Joyce and Impressionism," *Irish Renaissance Annual*, ed. Zack Bowen (Newark, Del.: University of Delaware Press, 1980), I, 13-31.

13. For a Wagnerian parallel, see William Blissett, "James Joyce in the Smithy of His Soul," in *James Joyce Today: Essays on the Major Works*, ed. Thomas F. Staley (Bloomington: University of Indiana Press, 1966), pp. 96-134.

14. See Erwin R. Steinberg, *The Stream of Consciousness and Beyond in* Ulysses (Pittsburgh: University of Pittsburgh Press, 1973), esp. Chapter 13, "The Sources of The Stream."

15. William Rubin's phrase, in his monumental *Dada and Surrealist Art* (New York: Abrams, 1968).

Chapter 2

1. *The Symbolist Movement in Literature*, intro. Richard Ellmann (New York: E.P. Dutton and Co., n.d.), p. 1. or Cf. Rémy de Gourmont—who had comparable importance in popularizing Symbolist theory in France—in "L'Idéalisme," in *Le Chemin de Velours: Nouvelles Dissociations d'Idées*, 3d. ed. (Paris: Mercure de France, 1924), p. 224: "the absolute is beyond our knowledge and cannot be formulated in symbols; what symbolism aims at is to display what is relatively absolute, to show the eternal in the merely personal." (This essay was originally published in 1893.) Books on the history of literary Symbolism are as many and various as its definitions. An interesting account of the difficulites of reaching a workable definition from manifestoes and statements of theory is to be found in A.G. Lehmann, *The Symbolist Aesthetic in France, 1885-1895* (Oxford: Basil Blackwell, 1950). Kenneth Cornell offers a concise history of the literary movement in *The Symbolist Movement* (New Haven: Yale University Press, 1951).

2. Two recent books on Symbolist art in English translation are Philippe Roberts-Jones, *Beyond Time and Place: Non-Realist Painting in the Nineteenth Century* (Oxford: Oxford University Press, 1978) and Philippe Jullian, *The Symbolists* (London: Phaidon, 1973). Unfortunately, Roberts-Jones does not succeed in defining what he means by nonrealist art, with the result that his examples seem diffuse. Jullian limits himself to French and Belgian Symbolism, thereby achieving a unity Roberts-Jones lacks but at the expense of comprehensiveness; Symbolism was a pan-European—even, more properly, an international—movement. Some of the best work on Symbolist art comes from Germany, with its now long tradition of *Zeitgeistgeschichten*. Particularly useful to me was Hans H. Hofstätter, *Symbolismus und die Kunst der Jahrhundertwende: Voraussetzungen, Erscheinungsformen, Bedeutungen* (Cologne: Verlag M. DuMont Schauberg, 1965), hereafter "Hofstätter S." Also extremely useful have been various exhibition catalogs of Symbolist art, some of which are referred to below, and such contemporaneous compendia of related work as the *Katalog der farbigen Kunstblätter aus der Münchner "Jugend"* (Munich: G. Hirth, 1916), hereafter *"Jugend,"* as well as more specialized studies of individual movements and painters.

3. "Définition du Néo-Traditionnisme," in *Théories (1890-1910) Du Symbolisme et de Gauguin vers un nouvel ordre classique*, 4th ed. (Paris: L. Rouart and J. Watelin, 1920). p. 1.

4. Part of *Les Fleurs du Mal*, in Baudelaire, *Oeuvres complètes*, ed. Claude Pichois (Paris: Gallimard, 1975), I, 7-81.

5. *The Symbolist Movement in Literature*, p. 5.

Notes for Chapter 2   111

5. On Art Nouveau, see Peter Selz and Mildred Constantine, eds., *Art Nouveau: Art and Design at the Turn of the Century,* rev. ed. (New York: Museum of Modern Art, 1975) and Hans H. Hofstätter, *Geschichte der europäischen Jugendstilmalerei: Ein Entwurf,* rev. ed. (Cologne: Verlag M. DuMont, 1969), hereafter "Hofstätter *J*"; also Maurice Rheims, *The Flowering of Art Nouveau* (New York: Abrams, 1966) and Robert Schmutzler, *Art Nouveau* (New York: Abrams, 1964). More specialized studies include Stephen Tschudi Madsen, *Sources of Art Nouveau* (New York: G. Wittenborn, 1956) and John Russell Taylor, *The Art Nouveau Book in Britain* (Cambridge, Mass.: MIT Press, 1967).

7. *"Jugend,"* p. 272.

8. Mauner, fig. 125.

9. *The Woodcuts of Aristide Maillol: A Complete Catalogue with 176 Illustrations,* ed. John Rewald (New York: Pantheon Books, 1943), no. 16.

10. Rheims, fig. 264. Cf. the same type of figure, though without the element of water, in a painting by Charles Filliger, *Child at Prayer,* in Charles Chassé, *Les Nabis et leur temps* (Paris: Bibliothèque des Arts, 1960), pl. 53, and also in a painting by Ferdinand Hodler, *The Chosen One,* in Rheims, p. 162. Cf. also archetypal representations by Gustave Moreau—*Narcissus,* ca. 1895, in *Odilon Redon / Gustave Moreau / Rodolphe Bresdin* (New York: Museum of Modern Art, 1961), p. 133—and Beardsley—*Hermaphroditus,* in *The Early Work,* p. 40. Cf. also the somewhat androgynous youth in plate 64 of *The Later Work of Aubrey Beardsley* (New York: De Capo Press, 1967); he holds a stringed instrument close to his body, and, like the fingers of the personification of Love in poem I of *Chamber Music,* his fingers stray upon it.

11. Pierre Daix and Georges Boudaille, *Picasso: The Blue and Rose Periods: A Catalogue Raisonné of the Paintings, 1900-1906* (Greenwich, Conn.: New York Graphic Society, 1967), p. 214.

12. Ibid., p. 215. Cf. *Sabartés as a Decadent Poet* (1900), p. 108. Also cf. a watercolor of 1904 which treats the subject of youth and sea in the conventional Symbolist manner, with a young man seated on the rocks, staring off at the sea: *Solitude,* Daix and Boudaille, p. 248. The portrait drawing of Junyer is probably a parody of a work by Puvis de Chavannes.

13. Cf. Minne's *Kneeling Boys at Fountain,* mentioned above. Hodler, who was one of the most important muralists of his time, termed such repetition "parallelism."

14. See esp. Robert Rosenblum, "Edvard Munch: Some Changing Contexts," in *Edvard Munch: Symbols & Images* (Washington: National Gallery of Art, 1978), pp. 1-9.

15. *Edvard Munch: Lithographs, Etchings, Woodcuts,* exhibition catalogue (Los Angeles County Museum of Art, with notes by Ebria Feinblatt, 1969), no. 26. An earlier version of this work dates from 1894. See Johan H. Langaard and Reidar Revold, *Edvard Munch: Masterpieces from the Artist's Collection in the Munch Museum in Oslo* (Oslo: Norsk Kunstreproduksjon, Stenersen, 1964), pl. 8. In this version the girl is faceless and is also fused with the sea in a way the girl of the later version is not. Munch was in the habit of reworking subjects in various media, some over a period of twenty years or more.

16. *Edvard Munch: Graphik aus dem Munchmuseum, Oslo,* exhibition catalogue (Hamburg: Ernst Barlach Haus, 1968), pl. 15.

17. *Edvard Munch: Lithographs, Etchings, Woodcuts,* pl. 25.

18. *Edvard Munch: Symbols & Images,* p. 43.

19. Cf., from the period of German Romanticism, Caspar David Friedrich's peopled *Moonrise on the Sea* (1823), in *German Painting of the 19th Century*, introduction and catalogue by Kermit S. Champa (New Haven: Yale University Art Gallery, 1970), no. 8.

20. In the introduction and notes to his edition of *Chamber Music* (New York: Columbia University Press, 1954). The Roman numerals in my text refer to these poems as they appear in the *Collected Poems*, in the Viking Press edition, hereafter *CP*.

21. "'His love,' referring now to himself and now to another, produces an oscillation of feelings, temporarily stilled by sound and tone, which prove to be less nearly final than they seemed at first. On second reading, the poem remains ambiguous" (pp. 94-95).

22. All references to *Stephen Hero* are to the New Directions edition of 1959, hereafter *S*.

23. *"Jugend,"* p. 77.

24. Cf. *Chamber Music* IV: "When the shy star goes forth in heaven / All maidenly, disconsolate, / Hear you amid the drowsy even / One who is singing by your gate."

25. *"Jugend,"* p. 75.

26. *Edvard Munch: Symbols & Images*, p. 51.

27. John Rewald, *Post-Impressionism: From Van Gogh to Gauguin*, 3d ed., rev. (New York: Museum of Modern Art, 1978), p. 187, hereafter *P-I*.

28. *P-I*, p. 285.

29. *P-I*, p. 284.

30. *P-I*, p. 283.

31. "The Sacrificial Butter," *Accent*, 21 (Winter 1952), pp. 3-13.

32. *WDaed*, pp. 63-64.

33. Agnès Humbert, *Les Nabis et leur époque: 1888-1900* (Geneva: P. Cailler, 1954), pl. 33.

34. *P-I*, p. 275.

35. *Oeuvres complètes*, ed. Henri Mondor and G. Jean-Aubry (Paris: Bibliothèque de la Pléiade, 1945), p. 366. David Hayman cites this passage as corresponding to Stephen's description of the artist's role in relationship to the work, *Joyce et Mallarmé*, (Paris: Les Lettres Modernes, 1956), II, 111.

36. *P-I*, p. 250.

37. See *P-I*, ch. IX, *passim.;* also George Heard Hamilton, *Painting and Sculpture in Europe, 1880 to 1940* (Baltimore: Penguin Books, 1967), pp. 50-55, and, in comparison with Munch, Frederick B. Deknatel, *Edvard Munch* (New York: Museum of Modern Art, 1950), p. 21.

38. *P-I*, p. 189. George Mauner has suggested this identification. This figure in *Vision after the Sermon* is not only the sole male in the row of peasants, he also resembles Gauguin. In this case Gauguin is imitating the Renaissance practice in which artists include themselves among the worshippers of Christ or the Virgin.

39. *P-I*, p. 412. Maurice Denis, in *Woman on Balcony (Marthe Meurier)* (1891), paints his face on a vase at the bottom of the canvas. See Mauner, fig. 74.

40. *The Early Work*, pl. 142. But cf. the same face in pl. 147.

41. Hofstätter *J*, pl. 26.

42. Hostätter *S*, pl. 50.

43. Cf. Albert Aurier in "Les Peintres symbolistes": "In the plastic arts.... No painter or sculptor worthy of the name is content nowadays with blear-eyed copies of social anecdotes, the fatuous portrayal of nature's warts, banal observation of the *trompe l'oeil* variety, the sterile ambition to be as exact and faithful as a daguerreotype. We have begun to envy the true artists of olden times their dreams and what I may call their wings. Even though we should fall like Icarus, we long to quit this muddy soil where the age wallows in its foolish presumption—to bathe in the upper air and explore the heaven of ideas, the spheres which are the dwelling-place of Symbols." *Oeuvres posthumes* (Paris: Mercure de France, 1893), pp. 294-95.

44. All references to *Exiles* are to the Viking Press edition.

45. *WDaed*, pp. 64-65.

46. The emphasis on contrasts earlier in this scene reaches Beardsleyan proportions, with color disappearing into black and white: "He could not see her face but he could see the terra-cotta and salmon-pink panels of her skirt which the shadow made appear black and white"(*D* 209). On 210, Gabriel is thinking of chiaroscuro effects.

47. *CP*, p. 51.

48. Rheims, pl. 488.

49. Hofstätter *J*, p. 252.

50. Hofstätter *J*, fig. 15.

51. Schmutzler, no. 113.

52. John Dixon Hunt, *The Pre-Raphaelite Imagination: 1848-1900* (Linoln: University of Nebraska Press, 1968), p. 178. Chapter Five of this study deals with the Pre-Raphaelite image of woman and makes some interesting comments on Beardsley's use of this image for satiric effect.

53. Hunt, pl. 4.

54. *The Artist as Critic: Critical Writings of Oscar Wilde*, ed. Richard Ellmann (New York: Random House, 1969). (The other painter dealt with in this passage is Burne-Jones.) In Mallarmé's poem "La Chevelure..." the flame of the hair would seem to continue in the eye: "L'ignition du feu toujours intérieur / Originellement la seule continue / Dans le joyou de l'oeil véridique ou rieur" (*Oeuvres complètes*, p. 53). An early version of the girl with long flowing hair is Lewis Carroll's Alice. His drawings of her—in the reprint of the 1886 facsimile edition of the manuscript of *Alice's Adventures Under Ground* (1864) (New York: Dover, 1965)—reflect Rossetti's "curious and fascinating type of beauty," but the real Alice, as the little photo on p. 90 of the ms. shows, had bobbed hair.

55. Hunt, p. 79, here quoting F.L. Lucas.

56. Mauner, pp. 224-25.

57. Roberts-Jones, fig. 116. Sometimes, of course, there are exceptions. Thus, in *Beata Beatrix* (Hunt, pl. 2) Rossetti gives us a figure with eyes closed, and in the *Silence* of the Belgian Symbolist Fernand Khnopff, the eyes are open, inviting the spectator to the moment of meditation (*De l'allégorie au symbole*, Brussels: Musées Royaux des Beaux Arts de Belgique, Musée Moderne, 1968, no. 25.) Lucien Lévy-Dhurmier (1895) sticks closest to the traditional iconography, with a figure with eyes also half-closed *(French Symbolist Painters: Moreau, Puvis de Chavannes, Redon and Their Followers*, Arts Council of Great Britain, 1972, p. 67).

Notes for Chapter 2

58. *Édouard Vuillard/Xavier Roussel* (Munich: Haus der Kunst and Paris: Orangerie des Tuileries, 1968), no. 199. This painting is also known as *Le Chemin*—the "way" or the "road."

59. *The Collected Works of Dante Gabriel Rossetti*, ed. William M. Rossetti (London: Ellis and Scrutton, 1886), I, 232. In the next stanza the speaker refers to the damozel's hair: "Her hair that lay along her back / Was yellow like ripe corn"; in the fourth stanza of the poem he imagines her hair falling over him: "Surely she leaned o'er me—her hair / Fell all about my face...."

60. Pierre Cailler, *Catalogue Raisonné de l'oeuvre gravé et lithographié de Maurice Denis* (Geneva: Cailler, 1968), no. 30. Rossetti's own version, done some three decades after he wrote the poem, has the traditional form of the vision with a female figure very close to the one in *La Pia de'Tolomei*, n. 56 above (Roberts-Jones, fig. 126).

61. "...elle a redressé sa tête, blonde et blanche, hors de la blancheur blonde des étoffes flottantes; et un fin corps *d'enfant féminin*, gracile, fluet et potelé; un invitant sourire, une promesse aux caresses, une mollesse inclinée à s'abandonner en des bras..." (Paris: A. Messein, 1925), pp. 120-21 (italics mine). The passage can be translated: "...she raises her head, blond and white, out of the blond whiteness of her floating muslins; and the sensuous and graceful body of a female child, slim and dimpled; an inviting smile, a welcome to caresses...."

62. *Mercure de France*, II (September 1891), p. 179. Quillard created a girl of this type in his play of 1886, *La Fille aux mains coupées*. See summary in Jacques Robichez, *Le Symbolisme au théâtre: Lugné-Poë et les débuts de L'Oeuvre* (Paris: L'Arche, 1957), pp. 490-91.

63. *Edvard Munch: Symbols & Images*, p. 49.

64. *P-I*, p. 271. This painting is known as *Nirvana*. Cf. also the ceramic *Eve* of the same period in Rewald, *P-I*, p. 410. The Eve in the *Exotic Eve* of 1890—George Wildenstein, *Gauguin* (Paris: Les Beaux-arts, 1964), I, no. 389, p. 150—is much more full-bodied than the *Breton Eve*. Wayne Andersen, in "Gauguin and a Peruvian Mummy," *The Burlington Magazine*, 104 (April 1967), 238-243, points to the relationship between the Breton Eve and a Peruvian mummy in what is now the Musée de l'Homme, Paris. This is an early instance of primitive influence on contemporary art. See also Andersen's *Gauguin's Paradise Lost* (New York: Viking Press, 1971), pp. 89-90.

65. *"Jugend,"* p. 212.

66. *"Jugend,"* p. 212. Cf. the Eve of the Belgian Symbolist Henri Evenepoel, in *De l'Allégorie au symbole*, no. 14.

67. Men as well as women show the same concern; Gabriel in "The Dead" checks his appearance in a cheval-glass (*D* 218), but, unlike Mrs. Mooney and her daughter, he is not pleased by what he sees. In *A Portrait*, Stephen, having refined away all that might bring life to his poem, also spends time gazing at himself in a mirror (*P* 71).

68. *The Later Work*, p. 21. Hunt comments on the relationship between the woman in this drawing and the Pre-Raphaelite ideal, p. 204.

69. On this association in art of this period, see Hanspeter Zürcher, *Stilles Wasser: Narziss und Ophelia in der Dichtung und Malerei um 1900* (Bonn: Grundmann, 1975).

70. *"Jugend,"* p. 9.

71. Cailler, no. 110.

72. *CP*, p. 59. Cf. "batlike soul" of the peasant woman who tempts Davin in *A Portrait* (183). See also W.Y. Tindall's remark on *Chamber Music*, XXXI, pp. 217-18 of his edition of the poems.
73. *Edvard Munch: Symbols & Images*, p. 44. Munch originally called this work *Love and Pain*. Cf. the much more explicit *Vampire* of the same year, in which a winged bat-woman is rising from the corpse of a man she has just killed, in Werner Timm, *The Graphic Art of Edvard Munch* (Greenwich, Conn.: New York Graphic Society, 1969), no. 3.
74. All references to "The Sphinx" are to page numbers of the version in *Poems and Essays* (London: Collins, 1956), ed. Kingsley Amis.
75. This image of Christ is anticipated by an earlier one, in contrast with that of Ammon: "Only one God has ever died. / Only one God has let His side be wounded by a soldier's spear" (149). Still earlier in the poem the speaker bids the Sphinx "Sing to me of the Jewish maid who wandered with the Holy Child, / And how you led them through the wild, and how they slept beneath your shade" (144).
76. Hostätter *S*, pl. 66. Hofstätter discusses the Sphinx and related types, pp. 187-200. The Moreau reference in *Ulysses* comes at the beginning of the "Scylla and Charybdis" episode (*U* 185.16): "The painting of Gustave Moreau is the painting of ideas." All references to *Ulysses* in my text are to the 1961 edition.
77. Hofstätter *S*, pl. 67.
78. Hostätter *S*, pl. 68.
79. Hostätter *S*, pl. 69.
80. Moreau's depiction was influenced by Flaubert's *Salaambô*. See Ragnar von Holten, *L'Art Fantastique de Gustave Moreau* (Paris: Pauvert, 1960), p. 19.
81. See chapter 1, n. 7.
82. *WDaed*, p. 33.
83. See Rheims, p. 404, in commenting on a lithograph by Wilhelm Volz.
84. Selz and Constantine, *Art Nouveau*, p. 72.
85. Langaard and Revold, opp. pl. 54.
86. Cf., however, *Chamber Music* V, where the young man is drawn from one room to another, from his room to the room from which Goldenhair leans out the window, "Singing and singing, / A merry air." Here, as in poem IV, where the young man's desire to enter her chamber for his visit is implied, the significance of the chamber, and his entering it, would seem to be sexual.
87. *WDaed*, p. 60. In *Stephen Hero* the scene occurs in virtually the same words and context; although it is written, like the version in *A Portrait*, from the viewpoint of Stephen, it lacks the vivid descriptive details of that version: "He thought of his own [fervid religiousness] spendthrift religiousness and airs of the cloister, he remembered having astonished a labourer in a wood near Malahide by an ecstasy or Oriental posture..." (*S* 156; the bracketed phrase was crossed out by Joyce).
88. *The Sacred and Profane in Symbolist Art* (Art Gallery of Toronto, 1969), no. 100.
89. Hofstätter *S*, pl. 18. *The Wood (Le Bois)* similarly may depict the Bois de Boulogne but symbolically depicts something else.
90. Hofstätter *S*, pl. 60.

Notes for Chapter 3

91. *Odilon Redon/Gustave Moreau/Rodolphe Bresdin* (New York: Museum of Modern Art, 1961), p. 154.

92. Note the flames, as in Sérusier's *Incantation*.

93. *Edvard Munch: Graphik*, pl. 50.

94. *"Jugend,"* p. 87. Cf. also Willibald Föhring's *Leipzig Winter Evening*, p. 80, and Sepp Frank's *March Morning*, p. 81.

95. Rheims, pl. 192.

96. Ibid., pl. 191.

97. Cf. Gauguin's similarly cyclic *Whence Come We? What Are We? Where Are We Going?* (1897), in George Heard Hamilton, *Painting and Sculpture in Europe, 1880 to 1940* (Baltimore: Penguin, 1967), pl. 25. The bed was also, for the Symbolists, a place of retreat, as in Vuillard's *In Bed*, fig. 1 above. In a letter to his brother Theo, Van Gogh comments on the famous painting of 1888 of his bedroom at Arles, emphasizing his attempt to suggest, through color, a place of rest: "It's just simply my bedroom, only here color is to do everything and, giving by its simplification a grander style to things, it is here to be suggestive of *rest* or of sleep in general. In a word, to look at the picture ought to rest the brain or rather the imagination.... The broad lines of the furniture also must express undisturbed rest.... The shadows and the shadows thrown are suppressed, the whole is painted in flat and large color areas as in Japanese prints" (quoted in *P-I*, pp. 210-11). Beardsley satirizes the whole notion of a retreat in a *Self-Portrait* from *The Yellow Book*, Volume III, in which he depicts himself buried in a huge canopied bed (*The Later Work*, pl. 24).

98. From "Le Tragique quotidien" in Maurice Maeterlinck, *Le Trésor des Humbles* (Paris, 1910), pp. 168-69. (Maeterlinck's essay began as a comment on Ibsen's *Solness*.) See the discussion of the significance of this passage to the Nabis in Mauner, pp. 251-54. In "Presences and Visions in *Exiles*, *A Portrait of the Artist*, and *Ulysses*," *James Joyce Quarterly* 13 (Winter 1976), pp. 148-62, I suggest how this concept of interior space influenced the dramaturgy and theme of *Exiles* and carried over into other work, including *Ulysses*.

99. *Edouard Vuillard/Xavier Roussel*, no. 33. Cf. The more naturalistic interior of Swedish artist Carl Larsson, Rheims, pl. 193. This interior of 1890 shows only a pair of folded hands (to the right) in an otherwise empty room. Cf. also Fernand Khnopff, *I Lock the Door upon Myself*, Rheims, pl. 155.

100. *Edouard Vuillard (1868-1940): Centiennial Exhibition*, catalogue by George Mauner (The Pennsylvania State University, April 7-May 12, 1968), no. 22.

101. *Vuillard Centennial Exhibition*, no. 8.

102. Cailler, no. 116.

103. *The Early Work*, pl. 63.

Chapter 3

1. *Cubism and Twentieth-Century Art*, rev. ed. (New York: Abrams, 1976), p. 15. I must express a general indebtedness to Rosenblum's interpretation of Cubism; his passing remarks comparing the Cubist achievement with Joyce's (and Stravinsky's) have been as helpful to me as his general interpretation of the place of Cubism in twentieth-century art has been. I am also much indebted to Dr. George Mauner of the Department of Art History at Pennsylvania State University, with whom I first studied Cubism, and Dr. John Neff, now Director of the

Museum of Contemporary Art in Chicago, for many discussions about Cubism when he was Curator of Modern Art at the Detroit Institute of Art. George Heard Hamilton offers a well-balanced history of the development of Cubism in the context of modern art in *Painting and Sculpture in Europe, 1880-1940*. JoAnna Isaak's "James Joyce and the Cubist Esthetic," *Mosaic*, 14 (Winter 1981), 61-90, explores certain philosophical relationships between Joyce's work and Cubism. A more general treatment of some of the same issues is offered in Wylie Sypher, *Rococo to Cubism in Art and Literature* (New York: Random House, 1960).

2. *Cubism and Twentieth-Century Art*, p. 14.

3. Urban as the subject matter of Impressionism frequently was, such subject matter fared just as well in nineteenth-century *genre* art or realism. In the work of Munch and of the German Expressionists, the urban setting is important for its psychological effect, consisting of largely unpleasant associations. In the work of the Futurists the city setting is important for its suggestion of technological advances and revolution. See Luigi Russolo, *The Revolt* (1911), pl. 109A in Hamilton.

4. One might also add Max Jacob and Pierre Reverdy to the list. See Mortimer Guiney, *Cubisme et Littérature* (Geneva: Georg, 1972). See also Gerald Kamber, *Max Jacob and the Poetics of Cubism* (Baltimore: Johns Hopkins University Press, 1971). The term "Cubist," of course, was used loosely in the early part of the century to describe a variety of avant-garde literary endeavors. LeRoy C. Breunig, "From Dada to Cubism: Apollinaire's 'Arbre,'" in *About French Poetry from Dada to "Tel Quel," Text and Theory*, ed. Mary Ann Caws (Detroit: Wayne State University Press, 1974), pp. 25-41, makes many useful distinctions on this matter in relationship to Apollinaire's work.

5. See especially Michael Groden, *Ulysses in Progress* (Princeton: Princeton University Press, 1977). See also Joseph Prescott, "The Language of James Joyce's *Ulysses*," in *Langue et Littérature: Actes du VIII Congrès de la Fédération Internationale des Langues et Littératures Modernes* (Paris, 1961), p. 306.

6. By the end of "Scylla and Charybdis," every view of the artist entertained or imagined by Stephen in the earlier work has passed again through his mind, but with greater irony.

7. *Aesthetic Meditations, 1913*, trans. Lionel Abel (New York: George Wittenborn, 1962), p. 14.

8. As Leo Steinberg remarks, "Curtains are pulled away on a catastrophic regression, parlor reverting to jungle and one flat brazen strumpet of simultaneous aspects regarding her clientèle. In their absolute presence Picasso's ominous whores stage a terrifying desublimation of art. The picture breaks the triple spell of tradition—idealization, emotional distance, and fixed-focus perspective—the tradition of high-craft illusionism which conducts the spectator-voyeur unobserved to his privileged seat." "The Algerian Woman and Picasso at Large" in *Other Criteria: Confrontations with Twentieth-Century Art* (New York: Oxford University Press, 1972; repr. 1976), p. 173.

9. See Robert Rosenblum, "Picasso and the Typography of Cubism," in *Picasso in Retrospect*, ed. Sir Roland Penrose and John Golding (New York: Praeger, 1973), pp. 49-75. These fragments of newspapers may also be said to suggest that art is as fleeting as life, and just as improvisatory.

10. "Picasso and the Typography of Cubism," p. 64.

11. See Herta Wescher, *Collage*, trans. Robert E. Wolf (New York: Abrams, 1968). See also Rubin, *Dada and Surrealist Art*.

12. In reference to "Cyclops": "The asides belong to a nocturnal decorum generated by a single impulse if not a single persona, a resourceful clown of many masks, a figure apparently poles

Notes for Chapter 3

apart from the self-effacing narrator. This figure may be thought of as an *arranger*, a nameless and whimsical-seeming authorial projection whose presence is first strongly felt in 'Aeolus,' where he starts usurping the prerogatives of the objective narrator by interjecting the frequently intrusive mock-headlines." "Cyclops" in *James Joyce's* Ulysses: *Critical Essays*, ed. Clive Hart and David Hayman (Berkeley: University of California Press, 1974), pp. 265-66.

13. In *The Widening Gyre: Crisis and Mastery in Modern Literature* (New Brunswick: Rutgers University Press, 1963; repro. Bloomington: Indiana University Press, 1968).

14. "...The Cubist sensibility to the kaleidoscopic assault of words and advertising images... represents the first full-scale absorption into high art of the typographical environment of our century." "Picasso and the Typography of Cubism," p. 75.

15. Hence the emphasis in *Ulysses* on the importance of events not depicted, but merely suggested, in the text. The classic example is Boylan's presumed seduction of Molly.

16. This line is often said to begin with Manet's *Bar at the Folies Bergères* (1881-1882).

17. See, for example, Wayne Booth, *The Rhetoric of Fiction* (Chicago: University of Chicago Press, 1961), pp. 323-36, though he focuses his criticism on Joyce's attitude toward Stephen and on the general structure of the novel, not on its imagery alone.

18. Stuart Gilbert, trans., *We'll to the Woods No More* (Norfolk, Conn.: New Directions, 1938), p. 5.

19. "Dans *Les Lauriers sont coupés,* me dit Joyce, le lecteur se trouve installé, dès les premières lignes, dans la pensée du personnage principal, et c'est le déroulement ininterrompu de cette pensée qui, se substituant complètement à la forme usuelle du récit, nous apprend ce que fait ce personnage et ce qui lui arrive...," Valerie Larbud, préface to the 1924 edition, p. 7.

20. Groden, Ulysses *in Progress,* especially pp. 101-110.

21. See especially on this subject Rubin, *Dada and Surrealist Art* (New York: Abrams, 1968), to which I am much indebted.

22. See portion reproduced in Kenneth Coutts-Smith, *Dada* (London: Studio Vista Limited, 1970), pp. 80-81.

23. Reproduced in Rubin, p. 73.

24. Tom Stoppard's *Travesties* notwithstanding, Joyce would seem characteristically to have stood outside the Dada movement while he was living in Zurich, but, as Walton Litz has suggested to this author, a study of Zurich newspapers of this period might reveal that Joyce could have learned enough from this source alone about Dadaism and other art movements of the time to have been influenced by them in various ways.

25. It is worth noting that the French *placard* refers also to posters, bills, and public notices, one of the prime sources of the collage technique.

26. Groden, p. 109.

27. On Futurism see Marianne W. Martin, *Futurist Art and Theory, 1909-1915* (Oxford: The Clarendon Press, 1968). Max Kozloff's *Cubism/Futurism* (New York: Charterhouse, 1973) makes useful distinctions between the two movements. Rosenblum has a chapter on the same subject (ch. 7) in *Cubism and Twentieth-Century Art.*

28. Cf. Picabia's *Amorous Parade* (1917), Rubin, *Dada and Surrealist Art,* pl. 33, or the bottom half of Duchamp's *The Bride Stripped Bare by the Bachelors, Even,* Rubin, pl. 19.

Notes for Chapter 3   119

29. The *Calligrammes* were published in 1917. See the *Oeuvres complètes,* ed. Michel Décaudin (Paris: Ballard and Lecat, 1965), III. The announcement of a public discussion featuring Apollinaire on the topic of the "Sublime Moderne" is a good illustration of the use of various typefaces and sizes in ordinary announcements of the period of World War I or shortly before. (See *Oeuvres complètes,* portfolio IV, item 1.) The avant-gardists built on this tradition, just as the Cubists, in collage, built on various traditions of folk art.

30. See, e.g., Marinetti's *Typomontage* on "Les mots en liberté futuristes," 1919, in Wescher, p. 58; this work was inspired by the manifesto of 1913.

31. Other possible influences on Joyce in this regard include the use of headlines in a similar context in some work of fiction preceding his, the use of headlines in a similar context in film (particularly in a montage sequence), or the influence of a type specimen book of the sort used by printers to demonstrate the potentialities of various typefaces. The last of these possibilities might be particularly useful to pursue in reference to the Dublin of 1904, if such books are still available anywhere. Headline sequences in film generally date from later than 1921 (see, e.g., F.W. Murnau's *Sunrise,* 1926), but there is always the possibility that such a sequence occurred earlier.

32. *Aesthetic Meditations,* p. 17.

33. This element in the composition, in fact, has come to be known as "Braque's nail."

34. Marinetti, *Selected Writings,* ed. R.W. Flint (New York: Farrar, Straus and Giroux, 1972), p. 41.

35. Wescher, fig. 53.

36. Wescher, p. 297.

37. Quoted in Rubin, p. 15. Rosenblum discusses *The Window,* p. 95.

38. "Resurgent Icons: Pound's First Pisan Canto and the Visual Arts," *Journal of Modern Literature,* 9 (May 1982), 159.

39. A. Walton Litz, "Pound and Eliot on *Ulysses:* The Critical Tradition," *James Joyce Quarterly* 10 (Fall 1972), 5-18, provides the critical context of the relationship. Robert Adams Day, "Joyce's Waste Land and Eliot's Unknown God," in *Literary Monographs,* ed. Eric Rothstein (Madison: University of Wisconsin Press, 1971), IV, pp. 139-210, treats in depth the relationship between the two works. All references to *The Waste Land* in my text are to *Collected Poems 1909-1962* (New York: Harcourt Brace Jovanovich, 1962).

40. Futurist drama and fiction—both of which anticipate in many respects Surrealist work in these genres—would not have inspired him any further. Marinetti's introduction to his novel *The Untamables* (*Selected Writings,* pp. 163-69) summarizes many of the features of Futurist prose style.

41. Marinetti, p. 41.

42. See examples in Hamilton, pls. 110A and 112B. *Wyndham Lewis on Art: Collected Writings 1913-1956,* intro. and notes by Walter Michel and C.J. Fox (New York: Funk & Wagnalls, 1969), reprints the manifestoes and other important documents of the movement.

43. Hamilton, pl. 118.

44. Hamilton, pl. 95B.

45. In Umbro Apollonio, *Futurist Manifestoes* (New York: Viking, 1973), pp. 27-28. On the distinction between Futurist aims and cinematography, see Anton Giulio Bragaglia, "Futurist Photodynamism 1911," in the same volume, pp. 38-45.

Notes for Chapter 3

46. Rubin, p. 33.
47. In "Ithaca," also, when he reads his father's letter (723).
48. "A Prayer," which dates from 1923, captures the *fin-de-siècle* tone (*CP*, p. 59).
49. See Rubin, fig. 20, *Fountain* (3rd version, 1964).
50. *Third Census of* Finnegans Wake: *An Index to the Characters and Their Roles,* rev. and exp. ed. (Berkeley: University of Calif., 1977), p. xi.

Bibliography

Andersen, Wayne. "Gauguin and a Peruvian Mummy." *The Burlington Magazine* 104 (April 1967): 238-43.
_____. *Gauguin's Paradise Lost*. New York: Viking Press, 1971.
Anderson, Chester G. "The Sacrificial Butter." *Accent* 12 (Winter 1952): 3-13.
Apollinaire, Guillaume. *Aesthetic Meditations, 1913*. Trans. Lionel Abel. New York: Wittenborn, 1962.
_____. *Oeuvres complètes*. Ed. Michel Décaudin. 4 vols. and 4 portfolios. Paris: Ballard and Lecat, 1965-1966.
Apollonio, Umbro. *Futurist Manifestoes*. New York: Viking Press, 1973.
Art Nouveau: Art and Design at the Turn of the Century. Rev. ed. Ed. Peter Selz and Mildred Constantine. New York: Museum of Modern Art, 1975.
[Aurier, Albert.] *Oeuvres posthumes de Albert Aurier*. Paris: "Mercure de France," 1893.
Baudelaire, Charles. *Oeuvres complètes*. Ed. Claude Pichois. 2 vols. Paris: Gallimard, 1975.
Beardsley, Aubrey. *The Early Work of Aubrey Beardsley*. New York: Da Capo Press, 1967.
_____. *The Later Work of Aubrey Beardsley*. New York: Da Capo Press, 1967.
Beebe, Maurice. *Ivory Towers and Sacred Founts: The Artist as Hero in Fiction from Goethe to Joyce*. New York: New York University Press, 1964.
_____. "*The Portrait* as Portrait: Joyce and Impressionism." In *Irish Renaissance Annual*. Ed. Zack Bowen. Newark: University of Delaware Press, 1980, I, pp. 13-31.
Blissett, William. "James Joyce in the Smithy of His Soul" in *James Joyce Today*. Ed. Thomas F. Staley. Bloomington: Indiana University Press, 1966, pp. 96-134.
Booth, Wayne. *The Rhetoric of Fiction*. Chicago: University of Chicago, 1961.
Breunig, LeRoy C. "From Dada to Cubism: Apollinaire's 'Arbre'" in *About French Poetry from Dada to "Tel Quel," Text and Theory*. Ed. Mary Ann Caws. Detroit: Wayne State University Press, 1974, pp. 25-41.
Cailler, Pierre. *Catalogue raisonné de l'oeuvre gravé et lithographié de Maurice Denis*. Geneva: Cailler, 1968.
Carroll, Lewis. *Alice's Adventure Under Ground: Facsimile of the author's manuscript book with additional material from the facsimile edition of 1886*. Intro. Martin Gardner. New York: Dover, 1965.
Chassé, Charles. *Les Nabis et leur temps*. Paris: Bibliothèque des Arts, 1960.
Cornell, Kenneth. *The Symbolist Movement*. New Haven: Yale University Press, 1951.
Coutts-Smith, Kenneth. *Dada*. London: Studio Vista Ltd., 1970.
Daix, Pierre, and Georges Boudaille. *Picasso: The Blue and Rose Periods: A Catalogue Raisonné of the Paintings, 1900-1906*. Greenwich, Conn.: New York Graphic Society, 1967.
Day, Robert Adams. "Joyce's Waste Land and Eliot's Unknown God." In *Literary Monographs*. Ed. Eric Rothstein. Madison: University of Wisconsin Press, 1971, IV, pp. 139-210.

De l'Allégorie au symbole. Intro. F.-C. Legrand. Brussels: Musées Royaux des Beaux-Arts de Belgique, Musée Moderne, 1968.

Deknatel, Frederick B. *Edvard Munch.* New York: Museum of Modern Art, 1950.

Denis, Maurice. *Théories (1890-1910): Du Symbolisme et de Gauguin vers un nouvel ordre classique.* 4th ed. Paris: L. Rouart and J. Watelin, 1920.

Dujardin, Édouard. *Les Lauriers sont coupés.* Preface by Valery Larbaud. Paris: A. Messein, 1925. Translated by Stuart Gilbert. *We'll to the Woods No More.* Norfolk, Conn.: New Directions, 1938.

Eliot, T.S. *The Collected Poems 1909-1962.* New York: Harcourt Brace Jovanovich, 1962.

Ellmann, Richard. *James Joyce.* New and rev. ed. New York: Oxford University Press, 1982.

Frank, Joseph. *The Widening Gyre: Crisis and Mastery in Modern Literature.* New Brunswick: Rutgers University Press, 1963; repr. Bloomington: Indiana University Press, 1968.

French Symbolist Painters: Moreau, Puvis de Chavannes, Redon and Their Followers. London: Arts Council of Great Britain, 1972.

German Painting of the 19th Century. Introduction and catalogue by Kermit S. Champa. New Haven: Yale University Art Gallery, 1970.

Glasheen, Adaline. *Third Census of* Finnegans Wake: *An Index to the Characters and Their Roles.* Rev. and exp. ed. Berkeley: University of California Press, 1977.

Gourmont, Rémy de. *Le Chemin de Velours: Nouvelles Dissociations d'Idées.* Paris: Mercure de France, 1924.

Groden, Michael. Ulysses *in Progress.* Princeton: Princeton University Press, 1977.

Guiney, Mortimer *Cubisme et littérature.* Geneva: Georg, 1972.

Hamilton, George Heard. *Painting and Sculpture in Europe: 1880 to 1940.* Baltimore: Penguin, 1967.

Hancock, Leslie. *Word Index to James Joyce's* Portrait of the Artist. Carbondale: Southern Illinois University Press, 1967.

Hayman, David. "Cyclops" In *James Joyce's* Ulysses: *Critical Essays.* Ed. Clive Hart and David Hayman. Berkeley: University of California Press, 1974, pp. 243-75.

_____. *Joyce et Mallarmé.* 2 vols. Paris: Les Lettres Modernes, 1956.

Hofstätter, Hans H. *Geschichte der europäischen Jugendstilmalerei: Ein Entwurf.* Rev. ed. Cologne: M. DuMont Schauberg, 1969.

_____. *Symbolismus und die Kunst der Jahrhundertwende: Voraussetzungen, Erscheinungsformen, Bedeutungen.* Colgone: DuMont Schauberg, 1965.

Holten, Ragnar von. *L'Art fantastique de Gustave Moreau.* Paris: Pauvert, 1960.

Humbert, Agnès. *Les Nabis et leur époque: 1888-1900.* Geneva: P. Cailler, 1954.

Hunt, John Dixon. *The Pre-Raphaelite Imagination: 1848-1900.* Lincoln: University of Nebraska Press, 1968.

Isaak, Jo Anna. "James Joyce and the Cubist Esthetic." *Mosaic* 14 (Winter 1981): 61-90.

Joyce, James. *Chamber Music.* Ed. William York Tindall. New York: Columbia University Press, 1954.

_____. *Collected Poems.* New York: Viking Press, 1957.

_____. *Dubliners.* New York: Viking Press, 1958.

_____. *Exiles.* Intro. Padraic Colum. New York: Viking Press, 1951.

_____. *A Portrait of the Artist as a Young Man.* New York: Viking Press, 1964.

_____. *Stephen Hero.* Ed. Theodore Spencer; new ed., John J. Slocum and Herbert Cahoon. New York: New Directions, 1959.

_____. *Ulysses.* New York: Modern Library, 1961.

_____. *The Workship of Daedalus: James Joyce and the Raw Materials for* A Portrait of the Artist as a Young Man. Ed. Robert Scholes and Richard M. Kain. Evanston, Ill.: Northwestern University Press, 1965.

Jullian, Philippe. *The Symbolists.* London: Phaidon, 1973.

Katalog der farbigen Kunstblätter aus der Münchner "Jugend": Sonderausgabe der "3000 Kunstblätter der Jugend": Ausgewählt aus den Jahrgängen 1896-1916. Munich: G. Hirth, 1916.
Kember, Gerald. *Max Jacob and the Poetics of Cubism*. Baltimore: Johns Hopkins University Press, 1971.
Kozloff, Max. *Cubism/Futurism*. New York: Charterhouse, 1973.
Kronegger, Maria Elisabeth. *James Joyce and Associated Image Makers*. New Haven: College & University Press, 1968.
Langaard, Johan H., and Reidar Revold. *Edvard Munch: Masterpieces from the Artist's Collection in the Munch Museum in Oslo*. Translated from German by Michael Bullock. Oslo: Norsk Kunstreproduksjon, 1964.
Lehmann, A.G. *The Symbolist Aesthetic in France*. Oxford: Basil Blackwell, 1950.
Lewis, Wyndham. *Wyndham Lewis on Art: Collected Writings 1913-1956*. Intro. and notes by Walter Michel and C.J. Fox New York: Funk & Wagnalls, 1969.
Litz, A Walton. "Pound and Eliot on *Ulysses:* The Critical Tradition." *James Joyce Quarterly* 10 (Fall 1972): 5-18.
Loss, Archie. "Presences and Visions in *Exiles, A Portrait of the Artist*, and *Ulysses.*" *James Joyce Quarterly* 13 (Winter 1976): 148-62.
Madsen, Stephen Tschudi. *Sources of Art Nouveau*. New York: G. Wittenborn, 1956.
Maeterlinck, Maurice. *Le Trésor des humbles*. Paris, 1910.
Maillol, Aristide. *The Woodcuts of Aristide Maillol: A Complete Catalogue with 176 Illustrations*. Ed. John Rewald. New York: Pantheon, 1943.
Mallarmé, Stéphane. *Oeuvres complètes*. Ed. Henri Mondor and G. Jean-Aubry. Paris: Gallimard, 1945.
Marinetti, F.T. *Selected Writings*. Ed. R.W. Flint. New York: Farrar, Straus, and Giroux, 1972.
Martin, Marianne W. *Futurist Art and Theory, 1909-1915*. Oxford: The Clarendon Press, 1968.
Mauner, George. *The Nabis: Their History and Their Art, 1888-1896*. New York: Garland Publ., 1978.
Munch, Edvard. *Edvard Munch: Graphik aus dem Munchmuseum, Oslo*. Exhibition catalogue with text by Isa Lohmann-Siems and notes by Gerhard Schack. Hamburg: Ernst Barlach Haus, 1968.
_____. *Edvard Munch: Lithographs, Etchings, Woodcuts*. Introduction by William S. Lieberman and notes by Ebria Feinblatt. Los Angeles: The Los Angeles County Museum of Art, 1969.
_____. *Edvard Munch: Symbols & Images*. Washington, D.C.: National Gallery of Art, 1978.
Odilon Redon / Gustave Moreau / Rodolphe Bresdin. New York: Museum of Modern Art, 1961.
Pecorino, Jessica Prinz. "Resurgent Icons: Pound's First Pisan Canto and the Visual Arts." *Journal of Modern Literature* 9 (May 1982): 159-74.
Prescott, Joseph. "The Language of James Joyce's *Ulysses*." In *Langue et Littérature: Actes du VIII Congrès de la Fédération Internationale des Langues et Littératures Modernes*, p. 306. Paris: 1961.
Quillard, Pierre. "La Femme-Enfant." Review of *La Femme-Enfant* by Catulle Mendès. *Mercure de France* 2 (September 1891): 178-80.
Rewald, John. *Post-Impressionism: From Van Gogh to Gauguin*. 3d ed., rev. New York: Museum of Modern Art, 1978.
Rheims, Maurice. *The Flowering of Art Nouveau*. New York: Abrams, 1966.
Roberts-Jones, Philippe. *Beyond Time and Place: Non-Realist Painting in the Nineteenth Century*. Oxford: Oxford University Press, 1978.
Robichez, Jacques. *Le Symbolisme au théâtre: Lugné-Poe et les débuts de L'Oeuvre*. Paris: L'Arche, 1957.
Rosenblum, Robert. *Cubism, and Twentieth-Century Art*. Rev. ed., New York: Abrams, 1976.
_____. "Picasso and the Typography of Cubism." In *Picasso in Retrospect*. Ed. Sir Roland Penrose and John Golding. New York: Praeger, 1973, pp. 49-75.

Rossetti, Dante Gabriel. *The Collected Works of Dante Gabriel Rossetti.* Ed. William M. Rossetti. 2 vols. London: Ellis and Scrutton, 1886.

Rubin, William S. *Dada and Surrealist Art.* New York: Abrams, 1968.

The Sacred and Profane in Symbolist Art. Toronto: Art Gallery of Toronto, 1969.

Schmutzler, Robert. *Art Nouveau.* New York: Abrams, 1964.

Steinberg, Erwin R. *The Stream of Consciousness and Beyond in* Ulysses. Pittsburgh: University of Pittsburgh Press, 1973.

Steinberg, Leo. *Other Criteria: Confrontations with Twentieth-Century Art.* New York: Oxford University Press, 1972; repr. 1976.

Symons, Arthur. *The Symbolist Movement in Literature.* Intro. Richard Ellmann. New York: E.P. Dutton, 1958.

Sypher, Wylie. "Portrait of the Artist as John Keats." *Virginia Quarterly Review* 25 (1949): 420-28.

———. *Rococo to Cubism in Art and Literature.* New York: Random House, 1960.

Taylor, John Russell. *The Art Nouveau Book in Britain.* Cambridge, Mass.: M.I.T. Press, 1967.

Timm, Werner. *The Graphic Art of Edvard Munch.* Greenwich, Conn.: New York Graphic Society, 1969.

Vuillard, Édouard. *Édouard Vuillard (1868-1940): Centennial Exhibition.* Catalogue by George Mauner. University Park: The Pennsylvania State University, 1968.

———. *Édouard Vuillard / Xavier Roussel.* Text by Jacques Salomon and Claude Roger-Marx. Munich and Paris: Haus der Kunst and Orangerie des Tuileries, 1868.

Wescher, Herta. *Collage.* Trans. Robert E. Wolf. New York: Abrams, 1968.

Wilde, Oscar. *The Artist as Critic: Critical Writings of Oscar Wilde.* Ed. Richard Ellmann. New York: Random House, 1969.

———. *Poems and Essays.* Intro. Kingsley Amis. London: Collins, 1956.

Wildenstein, Georges. *Gauguin: Catalogue,* I. Paris: Les Beaux-Arts, 1964.

Zürcher, Hanspeter. *Stilles Wasser: Narziss und Ophelia in der Dichtung und Malerei um 1900.* Bonn: Grundmann, 1975.

Index

Abstract art, 49
Aman-Jean, Edmond
   The Mirror, 26
Amiet, Cuno, 35
Anderson, Chester G., 15
Animism (in art and in Joyce's work), 33
Apollinaire, Guillaume, 42, 51
   Calligrammes, 53
   "The Cubist Painters," 44, 55
Arp, Jean, 51
△ Art Nouveau, 5, 7-8
△ Artist type (in art and in Joyce's work), 9-17
Arts and Crafts Movement (England), 8-9

Ball, Hugo, 51-52
Balla, Giacomo
   Dynamism of a Dog Leash, 62
   Study for the Materiality of Light plus Speed, 62, 63
Basilici,
   On the Tiber, 10
Baudelaire, Charles, 8
   "Correspondences," 32
Beardsley, Aubrey, 1, 8, 10, 26
   Les Revenants de Musique, 37
   Salomé (illustrations), 2, 17
Beaudoin, Paul Albert, 20
Bernard, Emile, self-portrait, 15
Boccioni, Umberto
   Unique Forms of Continuity in Space, 55-56
Braque, Georges, 49
   Violin and Palette, 55
△ Breton, André, 6
Burns, Robert, 21

Cendrars, Blaise, 51
Cézanne, Paul, 41, 49
Collage. *See* Cubism; also Dadaism, Futurism, and Surrealism.
△ Cubism, 5-6, 41-42
   aesthetic interest of, compared to *Ulysses,* 59-60

collage *(papiers collés)*
   defined, 45-46
   fragments in, 49
   headlines and captions in, 48, 51
   in literature, 42-43
   stylistic diversity of, 54-55
   subject matter in, 42
cummings, e.e., 42

△ Dadaism, 5, 6, 42
   Dadaist collage, 45; use of headlines and fragments in, 51-52
   machine imagery in, 53
   poetry of, 51-52
   in relationship to *Ulysses,* 64-65
Denis, Maurice, 8
   "The Blessed Damozel" (illustration), 23
   Le Bouquet Matinal, Les Larmes (Morning Bouquet, Tears), 26
   The Muses, 32
   Nos Ames, en des Gestes Lents (Our Spirits, with slow gestures), 36
   Le Soir Trinitaire (Trinitarian Evenings), 32
Duchamp, Marcel
   "L.H.O.O.Q.", 56
   Nude Descending the Staircase, No. 2, 62-63
   "Ready-Mades," 64-65
   Tum', 58
Dujardin, Édouard
   Les Lauriers sont coupés, 24, 50

Eliot, T.S.
   The Waste Land, 42
      Cubist principles applied to, 60-61
Exterior settings (in art and in Joyce's work), 29-39

Femme-enfant. See Symbolist child-woman.
Femme-Enfant, La (novel by Catulle Mendès), 24
Fidus. *See* Höppener, Hugo
Frank, Joseph, 46

Futurism (Italy), 5-6, 42
  collage, 51-52
  machine imagery in, 53
  "Manifesto of Futurism," 55
  principle of dynamism, 62
  in relationship to *Ulysses*, 61-63
  "Technical Manifesto of Futurist Painting," 62-63
Futurism (Russia), 62

Gallén-Kallela, Akseli, 34
Gauguin, Paul, 49
  Christ in Gethsemane, 15
  "Les Misérables," 15
  Portrait of Emile Schuffenecker and His Family, 16
  Portrait of Meyer de Haan (Nirvana), 25
  Self-Portrait with "The Yellow Christ," 15
  Still Life with Japanese Print, 17
  Symbolism in his work, 16-17
  Symbolist Self-Portrait with Halo, 16
  The Yellow Christ, 15
Geigenberger, Otto, 34
  The Sleeping Tree, 34
Girl with flowing hair type (in art and in Joyce's work), 18-33
  in *Ulysses*, 43
Glasheen, Adaline, 65
Gris, Juan, 55
  The Cups, 45
  The Table, 54-55, 56
Groden, Michael, 51-52

Hayman, David, 46
Hodler, Ferdinand, 10-11
  Spring, 10-11
  Youth Admired by Women, 11
Homer
  The Odyssey, 57
Höppener, Hugo (Fidus)
  At the Great Gate, 14
  Ausgeschlossen, 14-15
Huelsenbeck, Richard, 51
Hunt, John Dixon, 21, 22-23
Hyland, Fred, 21

Ibsen, Henrik, 29
Illusionism
  in relationship to Cubism, 54
Impressionism (in literature), 49
Impressionism (in painting), 44-45, 49
Interior settings (in art and in Joyce's work), 29-39

Johns, Jasper, 58
Joyce, James
  Chamber Music
    I, 13; II, 13, 37; III, 13; V, 19; VI, 31; XI, 19; XX, 20, 26, 30-31; XXI, 13; XXIV, 19, 31; XXV, 13; XXIX, 22
  Dubliners, 5, 9, 29, 30, 52, 59
    "Araby," 20, 35
    "The Boarding House," 9, 24, 25-26, 38
    "Clay," 26, 38
    "Counterparts," 22
    "The Dead," 2, 13, 20, 25-26, 29-30, 35, 38
      imagery in relationship to Symbolist art, 7
      narrative technique in, 17
    "A Painful Case," 13-14, 21-22, 30
      water imagery in, 12
  "Epiphanies," 9, 28
  Exiles, 9
    notes to, 18-19
  Finnegans Wake, 6, 12, 57
  Imagery
    chamber, 29-39
    Eve, 25
    forest, 29-39
    machine (in *Ulysses*), 53
    mirror, 25-26
    peacock, 1-2
    Salomé, 2, 26-27, 28-29
    Sphinx, 26-27, 28-29
    spotlighting in, 4
    water, 12
  Motifs
    artist as hero, 17-18
    artist as martyr (Christ), 15; in *Ulysses*, 44
    artist as necromancer (artist-seer), 16; in *Ulysses*, 43-44
    child-woman, 24
  "A Portrait of the Artist" (1904 version), 16, 19
  A Portrait of the Artist as a Young Man, 5, 18, 43, 58
    animistic dreams in, 33-34
    child-woman in, 24
    Cranly as John the Baptist, 2, 28
    eyes of wading girl in, 22
    girl with flowing hair in, 19-20
    imagery in relationship to Symbolist art, 7
    as Impressionist novel, 49-50
    interior imagery, 38-39
    peacock image in, 1-2
    solipsism of Stephen, 14
    spotlighting in, 4
    Stephen and portraits of Church heroes, 3-4
    Stephen as Christ, 15
    Stephen as hero, 17-18
    Stephen as *poète maudit*, 3, 9, 28
    Stephen's ecstasy in wood, 31-32
    temptress compared with Sphinx, 27
    water imagery in, 12-13
    women and girls in, 28-29

Stephen Hero, 5, 9, 14, 29, 37
"Tutto è sciolto," 20
Ulysses, 6, 18, 29, 39
 "Aeolus," 46, 47, 48, 50, 51, 52, 53, 56, 57, 58-59; use of headlines in, compared
 △ with Cubist and Dadaist practice, 51-53
 "Calypso," 63-64
 compared with *Les Demoiselles D'Avignon*, 41
 △ Cubist principles in, 42-60
 "Cyclops," 46, 47-48, 56-57
 △ Dadaist principles in, 63-65
 "Eumaeus," 47
 △ Futurist principle of dynamism in, 63
 "Hades," 46, 64
 "Ithaca," 47
 "Lestrygonians," 46
 "The Lotus Eaters," 64
 narrative strategy, 56-57
 "Nausikäa," 47
 Nestor," 63-64
 Nostos, 47
 "Oxen of the Sun," 47, 57, 59
 "Penelope," 35, 47, 59
 "Proteus," 43
 "Scylla and Charybdis," 43-44, 46, 52, 59
 "The Sirens," 39, 46
 △ sources of stream-of-consciousness technique in, 49-50
 Telemachia, 49
 "Telemachus," 46, 59
 use of fragment in, 48
 "Wandering Rocks," 46, 47
"Work in Progress," 6, 65
Jugendstil, 8

Kandinsky, Wassily, 42, 51
Klee, Paul
 Maiden in Tree, 33
Klinger, Max
 Beethoven, 18
Lacombe, Georges, 35
Lewis, Wyndham, 62

Maeterlinck, Maurice, 24, 36, 38-39
Magee, W.K., 16
Malevich, Kasimir
 The Knife Grinder, 62
Mallarmé, Stéphane
 Coup de dès, 53
 "Crise de Vers," 16
Marinetti, Filippo Tomasso, 51, 53, 55
Mauner, George, (quoted), 23-24
Mendès, Catulle, 24
Minne, Georges, 10
Modigliani, Amedeo, 51

Monet, Claude, 44
Moreau, Gustave
 Oedipus and the Sphinx, 28
Moser, Kolomon, 21
Motherwell, Robert, 58
Motte-Fouqué, Friedrich de la
 Undine, 21
Mucha, Alphonse, 8
Munch, Edvard, 6, 10; 24-25, 29
 Attraction, 12
 Jealousy, 15, 25
 Lovers in the Waves, 11-12
 Madonna, 24-25
 Melancholy, 11
 Starry Night, 12
 To the Woods, 34
 Two People (The Lonely Ones), 11
 Vampire, 26
 Withdrawal (Parting), 11
Music as supreme art, 37-38

Nabis, 4, 6, 8, 38-39
 interiors, 36
 version of Symbolist child-woman *(femme-enfant)*, 23
narcissism (in art), 26
nonobjective painting. *See* abstract art.

Pecorino, Jessica Prinz, 59
Picasso, Pablo, 9, 10, 49, 51, 54, 59
 collage of, 45
 Les Demoiselles D'Avignon, 44-45, 54
 popular culture in work of, 48
 variety of styles, 58
 The Window, 58
poéte-maudit, 3, 9, 15, 21, 28
Pont-Aven Group, 15
Pound, Ezra
 Cantos, 42, 59, 61
Prampolini, Enrico
 Spatial Rhythms, 56
Pre-Raphaelite woman (Rossetti ideal), 22-23
pure painting *(peinture-peinture)*. *See* abstract art.
Puvis de Chavannes, 8

Quillard, Pierre, (quoted), 24

Rauschenberg, Robert, 58
 Tracer, 56
religion of art, 33
Renaissance principles of form, 41, 55-56
Rewald, John, 15
Riemerschmied, Rudolf
 Eve and the Serpent, 25
 Summer Day, 25
Rops, Félicien, 8, 28

Rosenblum, Robert, 41, 48
Rossetti, Dante Gabriel
　La Pia de 'Tolomei, 21
Rouseel, K.-X.
　Maiden on the Path, 23
Rubin, William, 63
Russolo, Luigi
　Speeding Train, 62

Sérusier, Paul
　Portrait of Paul Ranson in Nabi Garb, 16
Seurat, Georges, 49
Shapiro, Meyer, 58
Stuck, Franz von
　The Kiss of the Sphinx, 28
Sumner, Heywood, 21
Surrealism, 5, 6, 8, 42
　Surrealist collage, 45
Symbolism (art), 5-6, 8
Symbolism (literary), 7
Symbolist child-woman *(femme-enfant),* 23-24, 25
　as a literary type, 24
　Nabi version, 23
Symbolist snow scenes (art), 34-35
Symons, Arthur, 7

Thoma, Hans
　Solitude, 9

Toorop, Jan
　The Three Brides, 29
trompe l'oeil. See illusionism
Tzara, Tristan, 51-53

Van Gogh, Vincent, 49
Vergil (Publius Vergilius Maro)
　Eclogues, 10
Verkade, Jan
　By the Seashore, 10
Victory of Samothrace, 55
Vorticism (England), 62
Vuillard, Édouard, 6
　In Bed, 4
　Interior, 36
　Mystery, 4, 36
　The Two Doors, 36
　Two Woman at Closet, 36

Wagner, Richard, 8
Wilde, Oscar, 2, 17
　"The Decay of Lying," 22-23
　Preface to *The Picture of Dorian Gray,* 21
　"The Sphinx," 26-27
Williams, William Carlos, 42

Yeats, William Butler, 1

OHIO UNIVERSITY LIBRARY

Please return this book as soon as you have finished with it. In order to avoid a fine it must be returned by the latest date stamped below.

JAN 5